1975.
oad

A HISTORY OF

THE HONG KONG CRICKET CLUB 1851-1989

香港木球會

Edited by Spencer Robinson

Introduction by Sir Denys Roberts

CENTURION

A Centurion Publication

76

CONTENTS

ACKNOWLEDGEMENT

The author is grateful to Alan Bailey, John Leader and Peter Davies for filling in many of the gaps; Bill Conway and Keith Garner for their help and patience; the staff in the Registrar General's Department and the Public Records Office; the South China Morning Post for pictures; and Julie Johnson and Malcolm Grubb.

A HISTORY OF
THE HONG KONG CRICKET CLUB
First Published in Great Britain in 1989 by

CENTURION BOOKS LIMITED
52 George Street, London W1H 5RF

Designed by Olimpia Wong, PPA Design Limited

Photocredits:
Many of the photographs were supplied by the Hong Kong Cricket Club; the origins of most of them are unrecorded or can no longer be traced.

The other photographs were supplied by, and are reproduced with the kind permission of, South China Morning Post Limited.

ISBN 0 948500 03 4
Printed and Bound in Hong Kong by
Paramount Printing Co., Ltd

INTRODUCTION

by Sir Denys Roberts

When I first arrived in Hong Kong in 1962, I was advised that I should join the Hong Kong Cricket Club as soon as possible. "They are not too particular about their members," I was told, "so you ought to get in."

The entrance fee was then $50.00 and the monthly subscription $12.00, though I was warned that there was a revolutionary group on the Committee which preferred solvency to a respectable level of debt, and that these figures were likely to be increased. Indeed, in October of that year the entrance fee became $100.00 and the monthly charge $15.00. A number of the 700 or so resident members found it necessary to resign in the face of this appalling impost.

It is worth noting that the total income of the Club when I joined was not much over $170,000, of which more that $50,000 came from the profits of the bar, which has remained a steady source of income although, understandably, some years were more unsteady than others.

The Club occupied its old premises in Chater Road, as it had done since 1851. Many of the younger members joined because it was central, it was easy to get into, it served the cheapest beer in town and it offered a set lunch at such a low price that nobody minded that it was inedible, save for the toast which was excellent.

During a short phase, which ended when the cook was found drunk with an Italian phrase book in his hand, continental cooking was in favour. The word "poisson" appeared on the menu with one 's' and the "sweet trolley" consisted of a blackened tray, suspended from a waiter's neck by a soiled cord and containing only liquified jelly.

In the year I joined, air-conditioning was installed in the dining room at a cost of over $20,000. It continued to work intermittently for some years, though the staff was often obliged to pretend that it had broken down, in order to get rid of those who dozed quietly all afternoon at their tables. Happily, the new clubhouse has a central plant, so that the entire building becomes uninhabitable simultaneously.

The Committee, which interviewed candidates in the top bar once a month, asked punctiliously if the new-comer played cricket. If he replied that he did, he was advised to put his name on a list, which was placed in the main hall and visited periodically by flies, though not often by the captain of cricket. If he said that he did not, he was admitted with enthusiasm, especially if he was a heavy drinker, since it would not be necessary to try and find a team for him.

The Club has always been careful to keep the entrance subscription at a low level, so that young arrivals, who seemed to have no difficulty in finding money for other pleasures, were able to join and maintain a proper balance between the athletes and the disabled.

I became a member of the Committee in December 1965, when there was a widespread belief, which still persists, that it did not matter who composed it so long as each was capable of reading whatever was in the beer-stained suggestion book which was supposed to be available in the lower bar. This often contained suggestions that members of the Committee should perform acts of incontinence upon one another, though I was assured that this was not why I had been elected (a word used to describe an unopposed appointment).

Until 1974, when the first professional full-time secretary/manager was appointed, the Club relied on part-time help, provided with more willingness than effect by members. Indeed, the words "relied on" are euphemisms, since one of the attractions of the Club, in its former home, was the cheerful incompetence with which it dealt with the majority of administrative matters.

In December 1972, I succeeded George Rowe who had already, as Alan Bailey recalls in the chapter on Wong

Nai Chung Gap, secured the firm support of the members for a move to new premises which were away from the centre of the city. It was therefore decided that, for a few years, the Club could afford to carry a president who would smile cheerfully at matters which he did not understand and leave anything difficult to the secretary/manager.

The Club has occupied its new premises for over 14 years. I doubt if anyone would now question the good sense of such a move in 1975. This was not the case 20 years ago, as can be seen in the chapter entitled "The Move"

Much of the opposition to the Club's tenure at Chater Road was somewhat artificial in origin and caused by a feeling that expatriates had been too successful in the past in reserving the choicest sites for their clubs and pastimes.

As momentum gathered, however, these feelings became too widespread to be ignored by the Government which offered to members an alternative site, formed for the purpose. In one sense, therefore, the provision of a new ground, allowing for its many attendant difficulties, was an act of grace, as the Chater Road lease was due to expire in 1971.

As usual, my own contribution was of little value. As a member of the Executive Council, I was asked to retire from the room while discussions took place about the grant of recreational leases after 1971. When I returned to the Council Chamber, nobody would look at me. I knew that a decision had been taken that the Club would have to move to the Gap. At the time, I thought that this was a serious reverse; I know better now.

I have thus watched the Club change, in the past 20 years, from being a happy place with air-conditioned beer, an unreliable lunch, a young bachelor membership and a central location. It has become a family centre, with greatly improved facilities of all kinds. Membership has increasingly been given to those with children, though recent committees have insisted on birth control being practised by candidates.

The old Club enjoyed a membership which varied from six to eight hundred and was prepared to elect almost anyone who applied, except those who were literate and thus looked upon with grave suspicion.

The present one has twelve hundred members and a substantial waiting list. And so, far from admitting anyone who asks, it only elects those who are likely to preserve the atmosphere of courteous incompetence which has been so carefully encouraged since the move.

There is a reference to Field Marshal Lord Bramall scoring the last century on the old ground. Apart from the fact that I contributed to this by dropping him twice while he was in single figures, I should like to remind readers that I was one of those who ran the first run at Wong Nai Chung. I made the mistake in the inaugural match of opening the innings with W.S.D. Barnes, well known for his cover drive between the legs.

The latter, who had decided in advance that he alone would be credited with the first run, refused to move during the opening over, when I twice steered the ball off the handle to fine leg for an easy single. It was no surprise to collectors of the improbable that he kicked the first delivery which he received to short leg and ran without looking or calling. I made my ground only because the fielder had found Barnes' conduct too funny to pick up the ball.

The booklet contains a well-merited tribute to the other sports which have become so important in the past decade. Among them is lawn bowls, with a laudatory comment on the manner in which players presented their buttocks to the public at Chater Road, though this is alas no longer necessary and is much missed by the nubes watchers. The squash section has done wonders in its new home with mildewed walls. Tennis has been played with much success on worn surfaces suitable for soccer, so much so that two permanent courts have been established which are available, in defiance of the weather, several times a year. The swimming pool, from which all water is removed for the benefit of children in November, continues to attract those who tear muscles rubbing in sun tan oil. Other sports are seldom to be seen at the new premises but this immunity is not likely to last.

Women have, in the last decade, had a serious effect on activities within the Club, as well as on members outside it, as was always the case. The admirable dining room, the excellent pool, in which the little ones can swallow water under parental supervision, the video club, where soft porn is greatly in demand by wives, the library, to which male members only venture after dark, and the many sports in which they take part show how important they have become.

On at least three occasions in the last quarter of a century, efforts have been made to amend the articles of association of the Club, so as to permit them to achieve full, or separate, membership. All these have failed, though perhaps it will not be long before their independent status is recognised, even if this will not alter their influence in the least.

There may be a few older members who look back with nostalgia at the old ground and conveniently forget its many disadvantages. Indeed, I notice a suggestion in the chapter entitled "Tourists" that I once took a catch to the disbelief of the crowd. The passage is inaccurate in that I did not believe it either, as it was not possible, at Chater Road, to hold something that has disappeared into a red coloured number 273 bus (Chai Wan only, of course).

But the majority will look with pleasure on the new Clubhouse and on all it provides. Before it lies a splendid future. ■

Denys Roberts

(Overleaf) The Chater Road ground in the early 20th century, looking north from Queen's Road.

FORMATION

By the mid 1800s, Hong Kong was established as a thriving port and strategic military base and an increasing flow of expatriates took up residence in Victoria and other parts of the 'Fragrant Harbour'. The military presence, almost inevitably, led to the introduction of various sports and leisure activities, and cricket was certainly played in the 1840s and quite possibly earlier.

The hub of Hong Kong's early sports scene was Happy Valley. Inside the race track most of the Colony's sportsmen rubbed shoulders and jealously guarded their own allocation of space. Cricket, football, polo and even golf were regularly played. For the golfers, stone setts substituted for holes to avoid irreparable damage, while a pond remained in the area as a challenging hazard.

The system worked tolerably well whilst the main users of the facilities were members of the armed forces. Their penchant for organisation ensured that the sports ground was used to its maximum efficiency. However, as more and more civilians arrived to increase the size of the business community, there was a call for increased sports facilities and the possibility of converting the Parade Ground on the seafront alongside Chater Road into "a place for public recreation" became a major topic of conversation.

In 1851, the area which had been drained and turned into a parade ground for the military, was described as being "a sloping dusty space in the winter and a muddy patch during the summer". The military felt they had a right to retain the land and tempers between them and the civilian community began to flare when it was proposed to build a new road (Queen's Road) running through the ground. The Government went out of its way to placate the military and even suggested diverting the road north along the water's edge but this was not sufficient to bring a peaceful end to the matter. On 12th June 1851, the China Mail reported: "A public meeting called by advertisment was held within the theatre (in Queen's Road East) on Saturday last for the purpose of adopting measures for converting the

HONG KONG 1889/90 OPENING OF SEASON

Reading left to right:—

Standing:— Sampson, ? , W. H. Wickham (*Electric Co.*), John Andrews & Dr. Lowson (*drinking*), Frank Maitland (*white tie*), Horsefall (*white straw hat*), (*B. & S.*), F. Lammert (*B. & S.*), G. A. Woodcock (*schoolmaster*) (*topee*), Beck (*Telegraph Co.*), Taylor (*China Sugar*) (*post*), Thompson (*Holiday Wise*), ? , ? , ? , ? , Leigh (*arms folded*), Taverner, Lt. Campbell (*arms folded*) (*Argylls*), Major Reynolds, R.A. (*slightly behind*), Sercombe Smith (*arms folded*), ? , ? (*slightly behind*), Dr. Atkinson (*arms folded, leaning*) (*post*), Hunter, Garfitt (*black coat*), F. Hazeland (*black coat*), Rev. Taverner (*cathedral chaplain*).

Sitting:— Capt. Festing, R.N., Beart (*B. & S.*) (*black bowler*), Bowles, Judd (*in topee*), Taverner (*post*), Drury (*P.W.D.*), Anderson (*P.W.D.*), ? , ? , Lt. Lee, R.A. (*afterwards Lord Lee of Fareham*), E. W. Mitchell (*afterwards President*), ? (*post*), Newton (*with bat*), G. P. Lammert, ? , H. E. Wodehouse (*father of P.G.*), Lt. Boyle, Lt. Young, R.E., Lt. E. M. Blair, R.E. (*famous army bat*) (*post*), Capt. T. Murray Rumsey, R.N., Travers with son (*Postmaster General*), ? , E. W. Maitland.

Hong Kong Cricket Club: Teams for opening match of the 1889/90 season.

present Parade Ground and vacant space on the sea side into a place for public recreation."

Some thirty people attended that meeting at which Mr. J.F. Edgar, MC, was elected to the chair and Mr. A. Shortrede, founder and former editor of the China Mail, was voted secretary to the meeting. The object of the meeting was then read out. It began: "That the sanction of His Excellency (Sir Samuel George Bonham) be obtained to the adaptation of the Parade Ground carried into effect on the opening of the new road by the waterside by levelling and turfing all the space from the upper part of the Parade Ground to the new road."

When the thorny topic of the Military Board of Ordinance's right to use the ground came up, Mr. W.T. Bridges, a recently-arrived lawyer and a keen cricketer, diffused the situation by proposing, "the adaptation of the Parade Ground, when not used as such, for cricket and other amusements". After more heated discussion about how the ground should best be used, Mr. Bridges' motion was put to the floor and carried unanimously.

Further discussion followed as to whether a club should be formed or whether the ground would be "thrown open". It was eventually decided that some sort of club be formed as the ground would have to be turfed and the Government was not prepared to make any grant towards the cost of developing the area, which Mr. Bridges estimated would cost HK$300. The chairman said that the Government would not give the land for private use so it was decided that it be developed for public recreational purposes.

It was also decided that the new club would be specifically designed to cater for the three branches of society in Victorian Hong Kong — the civil

Teams pose for one of the earliest photographs of cricket in Hong Kong.

(Left) Match in progress in 1860
(Bottom) Argyll and Sutherland Highlanders in 1889 on the Chater Road ground

professionals, the military and the tradespeople. At the founding meeting there was some concern that it was necessary to keep the membership of the club somewhat select. Mr. Bridges said: "For my part I have played with Tom, Dick and Harry at home and I don't mind doing the same here; but there is a limit to all things, and the new-fangled idea of a ballot system seems to be as good a mode as can be adopted if anything like respectability is to be kept in our social system."

Mr. Shortrede then moved that "a committee be appointed of the following gentlemen: Messrs Bridges, Antrobus, Smith and Lane, Captain Lodder and Lieutenant Chadwick, who are authorised to communicate with the Government and make such arrangements as would be necessary for carrying out the purpose of the meeting."

The meeting closed with a vote of thanks to the Governor and a double motion from a Mr. Phillips "that the committee appointed to make the preliminary arrangements submit their plans when matured to another public meeting and that a subscription list be opened at once."

The report of the meeting which appeared in the China Mail was not fully supportive and it concluded by posing the question whether the proceedings represented the wishes of the bulk of the community in the matter of "a place for public recreation and not simply a cricket ground." Nevertheless, that historic meeting held 138 years ago launched one of the first cricket clubs outside England; a club which has helped promulgate the sport in Hong Kong, ever since. ■

(Overleaf) The Parade Ground, looking north.

CHATER ROAD

The Chater Road ground served the Hong Kong Cricket Club for 124 years, from its creation in 1851 till close of play on 4th May 1975. Originally the Parade Ground, with the incorporation of additional reclaimed land, the ground was, in those early years, situated alongside the harbour front.

The first pavilion, a matshed in the north-east corner of the ground, was soon replaced by a more solid building, which was used until 1893 at which time it gave way to a larger building situated diagonally opposite, near where the old Bank of China stands. This stood for 30 years until what was to be the ground's final pavilion was built in the north-west corner. The opening, in 1923, of the new pavilion was a grand affair, with the Club's president, Mr. H.R.B. Hancock, officiating at the opening ceremony.

The pavilion was built of red brick and boasted an imposing entrance. It was light and cheerful and provided much more accomodation than its predecessor. It allowed members to watch the play from either the front of the building or from the spacious balcony. The changing rooms, described as 'splendid', included baths and there was a central hall where tiffin was served during all-day matches. The results of past Interport matches were displayed on the walls together with sketches of famous cricketers and the roll of honour of those members who gave their lives during the Great War.

In his opening speech, Mr. Hancock outlined the progress of the club. He pointed out that when the previous pavilion had been built it was thought that it would be too large and that the Club would never grow into it. Now, although it had served its purpose well, it was neither large enough nor modern enough for present requirements. He said: "Not many years ago this Club was not in a very

(Top) The second pavilion was used from 1893 to 1923.
(Left) The Chater Road ground in the early 1970s. The third pavilion, dwarfed by The Mandarin Hotel, was used from 1923 until the final closure of the ground.
(Bottom) 1925 aerial view, looking north. Chater Road ground on the right, Supreme Court and Royal Square in the centre.

good financial position and its membership was falling off. Thanks, however, to our late secretary, Mr. Hodgson, who devoted a tremendous amount of time, energy and skill going into all the details, we turned the corner and today we are, I think, in a very sound position."

The late Mr. Frank Maitland, president of the Club in 1921, had first suggested the new pavilion although a depression in trade at that time throughout the Far East meant few members could see their way clear to financially supporting the scheme to any great extent. The saviours were 'old friends', the Hongkong and Shanghai Banking Corporation, Messrs

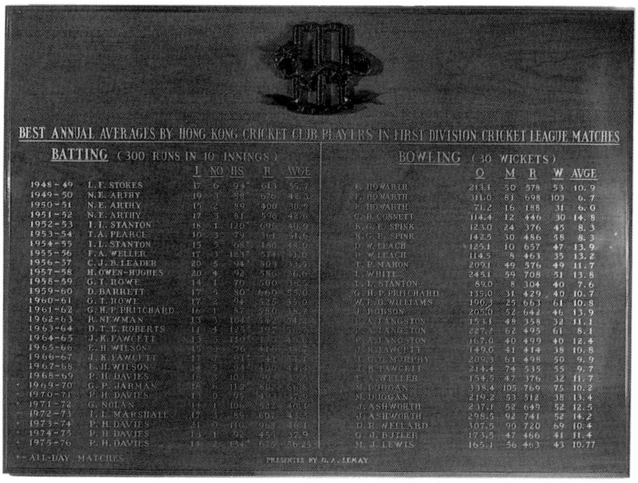

Cricket Honours Boards housed in Chater Tavern at the Wong Nai Chung Gap clubhouse.

Club presidents during Chater Road period: (from left) E.W. Mitchell, F. Maitland, Y.R.B. Hancock, H. Owen-Hughes.

Match in progress at Chater Road in the early 1970s.

Jardine Matheson & Company and the Union Insurance Society of Canton. Mr. Hancock explained there had been delays due to the previous year's seamen's strike and a general shortage of bricks. "I hope the young men in the Colony who are not members of this cricket club and who do not play cricket, when they see this nice building we have got will join the club and play," he said. "Most of us are getting too old and we must look to the younger generation to carry on and we hope they will keep the old flag flying for many years to come."

At that time the membership was around 500, with 248 resident playing members, and the list was growing each month. After being thanked by those present, Mr. Hancock said: "As long as I am able to stand up and walk about I shall continue to play and try to make a few runs on this good old ground." There followed a match between the Club and the Infantry.

The 1923 pavilion proved to be a very sound investment and was to serve the Club for more than half a century. In that time countless matches were played and, towards the end of

(Overleaf) 1910. Accession of HM King George V.

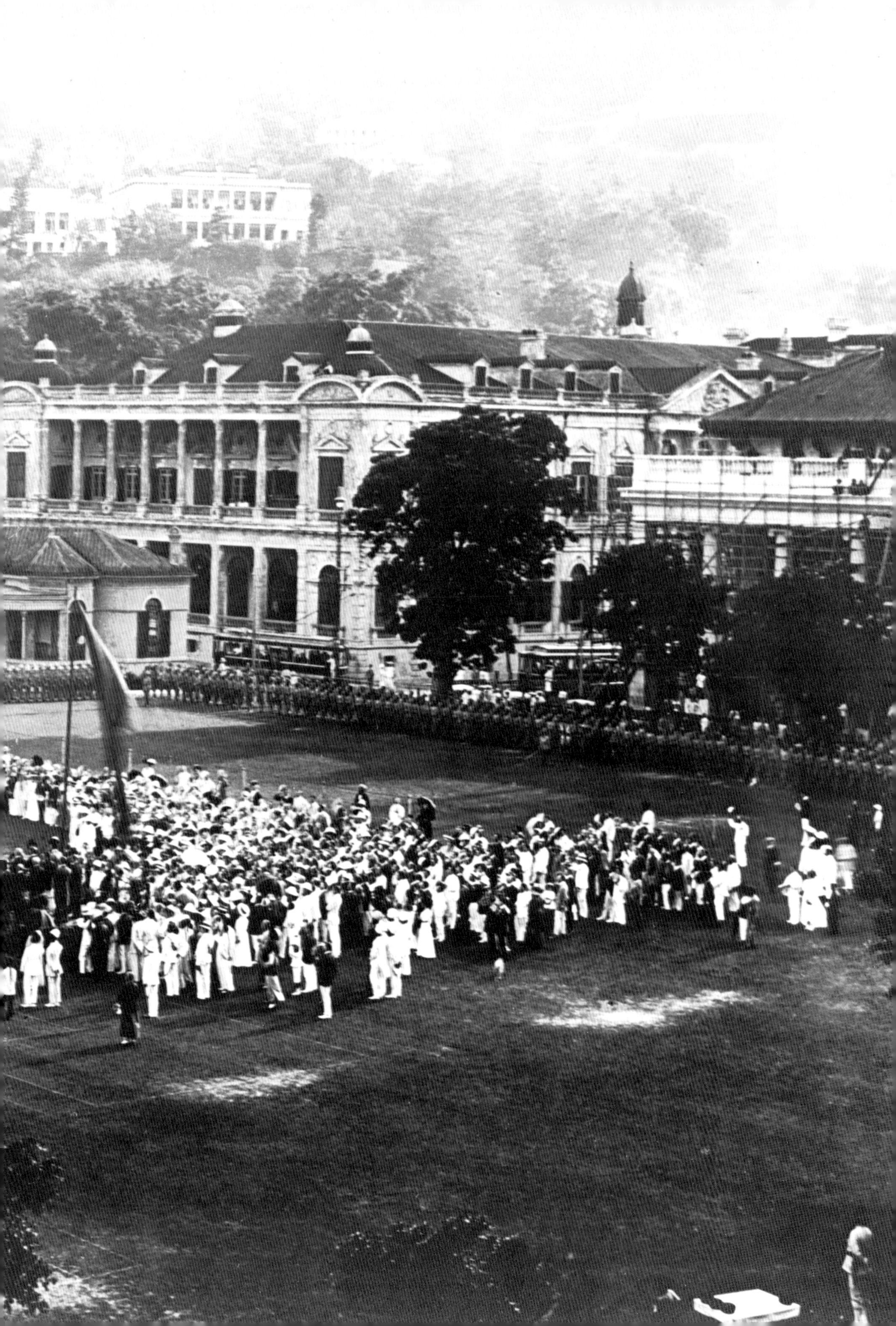

that period in particular, some of the sport's greatest names were to grace the ground. As a result, Chater Road became one of the most famous cricket grounds in the world and its unique setting in the heart of one of the world's busiest commercial centres ensured that it featured prominently in many journals, books and films.

Dudley Coppin, who joined the club in the 1920s and whose father had been a member before him, remembers that for many years membership of the club was based on 'rank' rather than cricket prowess and even recalls instances of outstanding players, who were not considered of necessary rank, being forced to play elsewhere. According to him, although potential members had to go through the motions of election they were, in fact, pre-selected by senior members of the British community, with the underlying thought being that members should be of the material from which future leaders of the Colony would be drawn.

Cricket ground to be thrown open

THE Urban Council will act as a "caretaker" for the cricket ground at Chater Road for an interim period of nine months, between July this year and March 1976.

Urban Councillor Kenneth Lo yesterday revealed that an official request had been made by the Mass Transit Land Acquisition committee to the council to take care of the ground as it will not be required until next March, which is nine months later than originally planned.

At the same time, the Hongkong Cricket Club had turned down the offer of an extension of its tenure and will move out to Wongneichung Gap this July.

"Any turf removed by the club to its new grounds would be replaced immediately by the council and the grounds thrown open for public use.

"The existing pavilion will eventually be demolished to make way for construction of the Chater Road garden, but its changing rooms and spectator facilities will continue to be available and part of the ground will probably be laid out as a temporary football pitch," he disclosed yesterday.

Traditionally, a member of the Cricket Club, on reaching the age of 30, would be invited to join the Hong Kong Club and once a member there would centre his activities around that club while still retaining membership of the Cricket Club. It was, in a way, a subsidy to the Cricket Club in that it helped to keep down expenses for the younger new arrivals.

The clubhouse, very much a male stronghold, was immensely popular at lunchtime and, while a high standard was maintained, prices were kept to a minimum. Even so, it was not uncommon, towards the end of each month when funds were low, for younger members to skip lunch, order a pint of San Miguel and enjoy the free cheese and biscuits placed on every table. "The stewards were very co-

(Facing page) Last matches at Chater Road; 3rd-4th May 1975.

LAST MATCHES AT HKCC CHATER ROAD
IN 125TH YEAR – 1851 TO 1975. R.I.P.

SATURDAY/SUNDAY 3/4.5.75

STANDING

AH CHOI, M. TRESS, "GEORGE", R. GIBB, C. TOWNSEND, C. STRACHAN, F. WALKER, R. KITE, R. COOPER, H. PATERSON, J. ABBISS, C. SHAW, B. NESBIT, (OBSCURED), E. CANNON, G. GLASSON, Mrs. COOPER (SCORER), J. VACCHA (UMPIRE).

SITTING

J. CORKILL, D. MINNS, D. GILKES, R. CAMPION, G. ROWE, W. TINGLE, A. BARNETT, T. SMITH, S. BARNES, B. HUGHES.

SITTING ON GROUND

P. BERRY, J. PHIPPS, J. LUNN, R. JOYNT, M. DUGGAN (SPRAWLED).

STANDING

R. ARCHER (UMPIRE), L. ROBERTS, N. HOOPER, G. TURNER, P. DAVIES, M. DEVRIES, R. MULREADY, M. SMITH, J. HUGHES M. ROBERTS, D. WELLARD, R. COOPER, K. SILLETT, A. BAILEY, P. GREEN, P. VAN VELZEN, B. HEMSHALL, R. DEWAR, G. FOSTER, J. SHROFF, P. HARPER, A. ZIMMERN, R. MILLS-OWENS, H. MELLOWES, (UMPIRE), R. SABNANI (SCORER).

SITTING

"GEORGE", P. LANGSTON, G. ROWE, E. WILSON, I. STEVENS, A. WELLER, G. PRITCHARD, F. ZIMMERN, J. LEADER.

NOT SHOWN

D. ROBERTS.

Match in progress in the latter days at Chater Road. View looking south toward Queen's Road with the original Murray Building beyond.

operative and kept it coming," recalls Ron Turner, who arrived in Hong Kong on Saturday 3rd November 1956, had his first drink in the Club on the following Monday and was elected a member one week later.

There were two bars in the clubhouse, one on the first floor (often referred to as the ground floor bar) and a men-only bar on the second floor. When the move was made to Wong Nai Chung Gap these were sold off and the first floor bar, together with its brass foot-rail, was snapped up for just HK$201, by long-standing members Robin Bridge and John McNie who, at the time, were sharing a house together in Jardine Terrace. After expenses amounting to many times the purchase price, the bar was moved and installed in their spacious garage where, according to reports, it was put to considerable use. When Robin got married and John decided to sell the house, the bar had to go and, by a happy coincidence, this was at just the time the squash players and lawn bowlers were starting to complain about the lack of drinking facilities near the changing rooms at the new clubhouse. And so the old bar returned to its original owners although it had to be reduced in length by almost half to enable it to fit between the two pillars outside the changing rooms. It stands today as just one more reminder of the past.

The curtain finally fell on "this good old ground" on Sunday 4th May 1975 with a game between the club 'Veterans' and 'Youngsters', the latter being those who had joined since 1960. Following the match the sombre ceremonies took place with members weeping unashamedly as the Royal Hampshire Regiment 'beat the retreat'. Sir Lindsay Ride, vice-chancellor of Hongkong University, took the salute on the top steps of the pavilion as the Club flag was lowered for the last time. A set of stumps and bails were set alight and the ashes placed in an engraved urn. The urn, in pride of place in a cabinet at Wong Nai Chung Gap, keeps the flame from 124 memorable years at Chater Road burning brightly. ■

The Hong Kong Cricket Club Ashes.

(Overleaf) Players in front of the first pavilion which stood until 1893.

THE MOVE

Few domestic issues in Hong Kong have ever aroused such widespread interest, emotion and bitter confrontation as the question of the Cricket Club's right to remain at one of the Colony's most sought-after sites. Controversy over the HKCC and its Chater Road ground, which dated back to 1883 when members of the public wanted the land for recreational purposes, reached a head in the late 1960s.

For almost a decade before the Government decided not to renew the Chater Road lease when it expired in 1971, the topic had become a burning local issue. It had long been an uphill battle for the Cricket Club, who finally learned on 8th March 1969 that their 118-year tenure at the ground was to come to an end. At a top-level Government meeting on that day it was decided that the ground would be turned over to the Urban Concil for development as open space for public use.

The inevitability of the news, and the promise of a grant towards the turfing of a new ground, did not soften the blow for die-hard members of the Club who had fought tooth and nail to hold on to what they rightfully believed was theirs. Although the announcement was greeted by Club officials and members with grief and disappointment, the writing had been on the wall for many years.

The location of the Club in Chater Road had been a controversial topic for decades. Arguments that it was an anachronism to have a cricket club centrally situated, and that the area could be better used by the public, had been the main point around which discussions had centred. Opponents of the move, however, claimed that the ground was already used by a large section of the community and that other central sites could just as easily be converted into open space for the general public.

Public clamour for the ground to be turned over to the people of Hong Kong had grown steadily throughout the 1960s as the topic blew into a major political matter. Local politicians latched on to the topic with great gusto. In many cases, it has even been suggested, they did so merely in an attempt to get in the public eye and see

MONDAY, APRIL 28, 1975

A fitting farewell to Chater Road ground

BY ROBERT TAY

Five hours and 29 minutes of glorious cricket under brilliant sunshine by Australia's Superstars of the last 50 years and the cream of the Hongkong Cricket Club, interspersed with ringing cheers from a host of club members and Colony enthusiasts marked a fitting farewell accorded to the Chater Road cricket ground yesterday.

The Hongkong Cricket Club will soon move to its new clubhouse and ground at Wongneichong and yesterday's match was the last major one on the historic cricket ground that has seen many a memorable battle between bat and ball for the last 124 years.

The Australian Superstars, flown here by Cathay Pacific Airways in conjunction with Ansett Airlines of Australia, specially for the series of matches starting last week to commemorate the closing of the ground have made the event one to remember not only with their presence but also with performances reminiscent of those in their greatest days.

And yesterday they brought the series to a memorable climax, treating the spectators to a display of superb, bright cricket as they successfully chased 237 runs for a four-wicket victory over the HKCC XI.

Stars of the side on this occasion were bowlers Peter Philpot who took five wickets for 54 runs and Jim Burke (two for 25) and Ian Johnson (two for 31) and batsmen Bobby Simpson (85), Rodney Marsh (46), Alan Davidson (36 not out) and Burke (36).

But the Chater Road ground would certainly not have rested in peace for the rest of its days had not its regular users produced anything in comparison. This satisfaction it did get with three great batting performances by Peter Davies, Noel Hooper and Peter Green and gallant bowling stints by John Ashworth and Roger Mulready.

Sent in to bat after losing the toss, Davies batted splendidly for a 68 in a first wicket partnership of 107 with Noel Hooper before being caught by Davidson off Philpott. Though slow at the start, he batted meticulously throughout his 83-minute stay, hitting 10 fours and giving two chances only after reaching his 50.

Ian Stevens scored only one run before falling to a catch by Ron Archer at fine leg, but Hooper and Peter Green continued the good work set by Davies, taking the score to 137 when Hooper, after a painstaking knock of 46, mishit to fine leg and gave Archer an easy catch.

Jim Hughes joined Green and earned a tremendous cheer as he drove Johnson past the midwicket boundary but in stepping back to make the stroke he hit the wicket and was out instead for a duck. Four wickets were now down for 135.

Peter Green by this time was getting his eye in and driving forcefully all round the wicket. He lost Martin Bulfied, caught behind the wicket for 10 runs, Roger Mulready, also caught behind the wicket for a "duck", but fours flowed off his bat as well as two sixes as he pummelled the bowling to roar past his 50 and take the score to 183 for six.

Geoff Foster stayed 36 minutes for a 12 to help take the score to 234, as Green raced to his 86 and then skied into the gully to give an easy catch.

John Ashworth, next in, stepped out to turn a Lindwall delivery to leg, missed, and before he could recover, his stumps were shattered by the wicketkeeper.

Dave Wellard joined Green and took a single, giving Green the strike. Two fours and a single saw Green reach his 95, but in trying to reach his century he stepped out to the first ball of the next over, completely missed and was clean bowled.

SCOREBOARD

HKCC

P. Davies, c Davidson b Philpott	68
N. Hooper, c Archer b Johnson	46
I. Stevens, c Archer b Philpott	1
P. Green, b Philpott	95
J. Hughes, hit wkt b Johnson	0
M. Bulfield, c Marsh b Philpott	10
R. Mulready, c Marsh b Philpott	0
G. Foster, c Harvey b Burke	12
J. Ashworth, st Marsh b Burke	0
D. Wellard, not out	1
Extras	3
Total (for 9 wkts decl)	236

Did not bat: P. Francis.

Fall of Wickets: 1-107, 2-109, 3-137, 4-135, 5-183, 6-183, 7-234, 8-234, 9-236.

BOWLING ANALYSIS

	O	M	R	W
R. Lindwall	6	0	10	0
A. Davidson	9	2	27	0
R. Archer	7	0	40	0
P. Philpott	16.1	2	54	5
J. Burke	9	0	25	2
I. Johnson	4	0	31	2
R. Simpson	10	2	46	0

SUPERSTARS

J. Burke, b Ashworth	36
H. Simpson, b Ashworth	85
N. Harvey, b Ashworth	5
L. Favell, c Foster b Mulready	16
I. Craig, c Hooper b Mulready	3
R. Marsh, c Davies b Mulready	46
A. Davidson, not out	36
P. Philpott, not out	6
Extras	4
Total (for 6 wkts)	237

Did not bat: R. Archer, R. Lindwall, I. Johnson.

Fall of Wickets: 1-105, 2-123, 3-130, 4-139, 5-157, 6-220

BOWLING ANALYSIS

	O	M	R	W
D. Wellard	8	2	41	0
P. Francis	5	1	32	0
J. Ashworth	17	0	70	3
J. Hughes	4	0	32	0
R. Mulready	10	0	57	3
P. Davies	2	0	1	0

His 95, compiled in even time, was a magnificent one filled with delightful mighty drives all round the wicket and except for one "life," when he was dropped by Marsh behind the wicket, was a chanceless one.

With his departure the innings closed at 236 for nine declared.

The Superstars opened with Jim Burke and Bobby Simpson to the bowling of Dave Wellard and Paul Francis.

Both played cautiously for the half hour before tea, taking the score to 27 for no wicket. Fours began to flow after tea as Simpson got into his stride with well-timed leg pulls and off-drives and Burke repeatedly steered his shots through the gully or past fine-leg.

The partnership reached 105 when Burke was bowled by Ashworth. Neil Harvey contributed five runs, then also fell to Ashworth and the Superstars were two out for 123. Seven runs later Ashworth struck again, this time clean bowling Simpson after the ex-Australian captain had scored 85 runs, including 18 fours.

Inspired by these successes, the HKCC, backed by some very fine fielding, had Les Favell caught for 16 and Ian Craig for three and looked well in the fight.

But any hopes of victory by them were gradually shattered when Alan Davidson came in to join Rodney March. Both began to dominate the bowling and, refusing to lift the ball to the spread out field, kept the scoreboard moving with singles.

As time started to run out, both went for big hits and March supplied the fireworks with five fours and two sixes – one over the screen and the other a mighty one over the club pavilion. Trying for another six he mistimed and was held by Peter Davies near the long-off boundary. But by then his 46 had brought the total to 220 for six and the team well within reach of victory.

Davidson and Philpott took the score to 236 with singles and then with the Superstars needing only one run for victory HKCC skipper Peter Davies put himself to bowl.

But the match was not to end without a humorous touch. Trying a big hit for the winning run, Davidson lost grip of the bat, sending it flying yards away, amidst loud laughter from the crowd. He took out his handkerchief, wrappeo it round the handle and succeeded in connecting with the next ball for the needed single.

Former Australian Test skipper Bobby Simpson turns one to leg in his magnificent knock of 85 for the Superstars against the HKCC XI at Chater Road yesterday.

View of Chater Road ground from the Hilton Hotel.

their names prominently displayed and constantly in the limelight.

It was in August, 1961 that Urban Councillor Hilton Cheong-leen accused the Town Planning Board of "side stepping the so-called controversial issue" of the HKCC ground, stating that "For this purpose (public open space), the present Hong Kong Cricket Club ground would be suitable as it is fairly large and is easily accessible to the public."

Cheong-leen went on to say that most people had agreed that the Cricket Club be removed from the Chater Road area. One suggestion put forward was that the Club could be moved to the site opposite the Queen Victoria Park in Causeway Bay, which at the time was occupied by the military authorities.

Following is the sequence of events leading to Government's decision to turn the Chater Road ground over to the Urban Council for development as open space for public use.

18th March 1963: Mr. Y.K. Kan proposed in a Legislative Council meeting that the Government should turn the Club ground into either a site for public recreation or a multi-storey car park. Kan, an Unofficial member of the Council, said there was no logical reason why a small private club should be given exclusive possession and use of one of the most valuable plots of land right in the heart of the city. "The cricket ground is not fully used except for a game of cricket at weekends and some tennis matches at other times," he said, and went on: "For the rest of the time it is just an open space but barred to all-comers."

19th March 1963: John Leader, Secretary of the HKCC, said he was in favour of a car park being built below the Chater Road ground. "I think it would be a great answer to the city's parking problem," said Leader, who nevertheless doubted the feasibility of the project. He denied Y.K. Kan's allegations that the Club was "barred to all-comers" and said the Club playground was open to the public who would like to watch the sports activities inside. "Quite a lot of social activities are being conducted on the Club ground every year," he said.

THE STAR, Hongkong, Tuesday, April 29, 1975. Page 9.

CRICKET GROUND TO BECOME QUEEN'S SQ

THE Hongkong Cricket Club ground in Central will soon be turned into a permanent park, reliable sources said today.

Earlier plans to use it as a worksite for construction works on our underground railway have been scrapped, the sources said.

Instead work to turn the grounds into a modern "green lung" for thousands of Central workers will start as soon as the Club's lease runs out in July, the sources reported.

Another site will have to be found by the Mass Transit Railway Authority for its building works.

The recent decision by the government — which is a reversal on its plans — is expected to be announced to coincide with the Queen's visit which starts on Sunday.

It has been named Queen's Square or Queen's Garden, it was said.

The chairman of the Urban Council's recreations and amenities select committee, Mr Kenneth T.C. Lo, said he had also heard of the new government decision on the grounds.

"It's not official yet — in other words the Council has not been officially informed by the Government," Mr Lo said.

He said he heard of the plan "recently" but would not say from where he heard it. "I cannot say anything now," he said.

A Council spokesman, welcomed the news.

"We hope Queen's Square will be built according to the very pleasing and ambitious plans the Council approved some years ago when the project was to become Chater Road Garden," he said.

The Mass Transit had recently asked the Urban Council to act as a caretaker of the grounds until it takes over nine months after the club evacuates its site.

A soccer pitch was to be built on the grounds and the spectators stand was to remain until March 26 next year, when the Mass Transit was to take over.

Changing rooms and part of the grounds were to be open to the public.

"A SLIGHT ALTERATION TO THE RULES, OLD MAN, AND IT WAS EASY."

"It might even be possible to build a large car park below it or even on it (Hongkong Cricket Club) without detracting from the amenities the ground can offer." — Mr Y. K. Kan

28th March 1963: Speaking at a Legislative Council meeting, the Colonial Secretary, the Hon. E.B. Teesdale, said there would eventually come a time when the Government would have to find a "less central site" for the Cricket Club. He said while there is still some balance of the lease to run the Government should start thinking about where the ground should be relocated.

17th April 1963: A suggestion that the Club be given an alternative site on Causeway Bay land released by the Army was made to the Government through the Urban Council. The Government replied that the proposal would be considered at the appropriate time.

2nd January 1965: A newspaper report, quoting an unnamed source, said the Club was ready to give up the Chater Road ground and move to a new site at Wong Nai Chung Gap Road.

3rd January 1965: Donald Leach, president of the Club, denied the report that the Club had decided to give up Chater Road for a new location. "The Club has not discussed this question at any committee meeting," he said. John Leader added: "I've never heard anything about it."

7th January 1965: A Hongkong Standard report claimed the Government was speeding up development of land for the Cricket Club at the top of Wong Nai Chung Gap Road. The site, near the St. John's Cenotaph, will be given to the Club in exchange for the Chater Road ground, said the report, which added that the site was earmarked for the Club in the Public Works Department private file. According to the report, development work on the site had begun in 1963 and Club officials had agreed to a move at a private meeting with Government heads although nothing was put in writing.

8th January 1965: A Government spokesman said the plan to provide for the Club in the eastern playing field area of the Central Town Planning Redevelopment Scheme, should the Club be required to give up the Chater Road ground, had not changed. He

said the Government had not entered into any agreement with the Club with regard to a future site.

19th January 1965: The Hon. Y.K. Kan said he would bring up the topic of re-siting of the Cricket Club at a Legislative Council meeting. He said he would ask the Government if it had given consideration to the matter of coming up with an alternative home, and in the event that a suitable site was available he said he would also ask "if it is the Government's intention to effect the exchange immediately rather than wait until the present lease runs out." He continued: "Will Government give this Council the assurance that we will be kept closely informed of any negotiations, and also that we will be consulted before any final decision is taken as to the alternative site."

20th January 1965: Replying to questions by Mr. Y.K. Kan, the Hon. E.B. Teesdale, the Colonial Secretary, told the Legislative Council that the Government had no plans at present to negotiate an immediate exchange for the re-siting of the Cricket Club. Mr. Teesdale said the Government had not reached any conclusion on what should be done with the Cricket Club if it was decided to re-site it. "There has been no consultation or negotiation with the Club, and there is no present intention to negotiate an immediate exchange", he said. Mr. Teesdale made it clear that the Government would keep the Council informed of any developments on the matter.

11th February 1966: An Advisory Committee was set up by the Government to review its existing policy on private recreational leases so that all clubs might be given ample notice of any changes. Until then the Government's policy had been based on the recommendations in the Morse Report of 1949-50, which proposed a system of 10- and 21-year leases, the first of which were granted to run from 25th December 1951.

3rd October 1967: Mr. D.J.R. Blaker, the Urban Council's newest appointed member, revived the question of whether the HKCC ground should be

opened to the public. He asked about Government plans for the public land in Central and requested that Government be asked to consider the premises of the Club.

6th August 1968: An Urban Council motion on open space in the Central area of Hong Kong developed into a lengthy, and often strongly-worded debate around the re-siting of the HKCC. The motion, moved by Mr. Hilton Cheong-leen and seconded by Mr. D.J.R. Blaker, was that the Council urge the Government to provide more public open space in the Central district. However, despite detailed accounts of both sides of the case being put forward, no decision was reached and an amendment suggested by Mr. A. de O. Sales, Chairman of the Recreation and Amenities Select Committee, was accepted by all the councillors. The Council decided, rather than force members to vote, to refer the motion to a joint meeting of the Museum and Art Gallery Select Committee and the Recreation and Amenities Select Committee for their consideration.

According to a newspaper report, one side of the debate favoured reserving the ground for public open space after the lease expired. The other side rejected this and argued that other districts in the Colony deserved attention in this regard before Central. Mr. Cheong-leen said the 1968 report of the Advisory Committee on Private Recreational leases recommended the Cricket Club should be granted a fresh

Page 18, THE STAR, Hongkong, Monday, May 5, 1975.

A day of nostalgia

THE Hongkong Cricket Club officially closed its ground in Chater Road yesterday as the Royal Hampshire Regiment "beat the retreat".

Prior to the closing ceremony, the club veterans played a friendly match against a team of youngsters.

The Youngsters who made a team of players who joined the club after 1960, had the better of the Old Timers with one wicket to spare after scoring 250 runs.

Ian Stevens stole the show with 67 runs not out to help the Youngsters edge out the Old Timers whose best batsman was Neil Hooper with 56 runs.

● Picture above shows the Royal Hampshire Regiment "beating the retreat" at the Hongkong Cricket Club yesterday.

Page 14, THE STAR, Hongkong, Saturday, April 26, 1975.

Final week-end for cricket ground

The visiting "greats" of Australian Test cricket wind up their lightning tour to mark the closing of the Hongkong Cricket Club ground with two matches this weekend.

At the Chater Club Road ground Ian Johnston's Australian Cathay-Rothman's "Superstars" will mix with a combined Hongkong team in what promises to be a great day's entertainment.

The first ball will be bowled on the 124-year-old ground at 11 am.

The Australian stars of yesteryear — and of course the present Australian Test team's wicket keeping ace Rodney Marsh — should blend in nicely with the Hongkong boys for a big hitting day.

Bowlers

Bowlers such as Allan Davidson and Ray Lindwall are expected to be on opposing sides this afternoon while the batting strength of Neil Harvey, Jim Burke, Rodney Marsh and former Australian Test captain Ian Craig will be split up evenly on each side with Hongkong's top cricketers.

The final match of the successful tour starts at 11.30 am tomorrow when a top Hongkong XI captained by Peter Davies meets the visitors for the final game on the old ground before the club moves its quarters to Wongneichong Gap Road.

lease in 1971 for a term of ten years. However, he said: "The City Hall and Statue Square have become the cultural heart of Hong Kong. We need to expand this cultural heart and we can best do so by turning the Cricket Club ground into public open space." Seconding the motion, Mr. Blaker said conditions had changed entirely from the time when the Club originally took up its position on the edge of what was then a relatively small village. "It is now in the midst of a thriving, bustling city. I hardly think that is a symbol that the majority of our community would choose to have as its city square." he said.

Opposing the motion, Mr. Kenneth Lo and Mr. Gerry Forsgate said the Council's attention was being misdirected. Both argued that other districts in Hong Kong were in more urgent need of open space and that Central was relatively well provided for. Mr. Lo said that if the grounds of clubs and associations were taken away, organised sport in Hong Kong would be destroyed.

13th February 1969: Mr. Raymond Kan, an architect and a candidate for the Urban Council elections in March, called for the removal of the Cricket Club from Central. A Civic Association candidate, he said the ground should be replaced by an underground car park and a museum and art gallery with a roof-top garden.

8th March 1969: The Government decided not to renew the lease of the Club's Chater Road ground when it expired in 1971. It was agreed to turn the ground over to the Urban Council for development as open space for public use. Legislative Councillor Mrs. Ellen Li Shu-pui said: "It has been a political issue for some time. It is disappointing that we have had to have racial discrimination in the centre of town. The Cricket Club is symbolic of discrimination," she said.

The Government offered the Cricket Club a 146,000 square-foot site at Wong Nai Chung Gap Road and a HK$40,000 grant towards the cost of turfing the new ground. "It is a small concession to help soften the natural disappointment felt by the Club at having to break its historical connection with the present ground," said a Government spokesman. ■

WONG NAI CHUNG GAP

The twelve months following the verdict were times of worry and uncertainty for the Cricket Club. Threats of resignation from a large section of the membership cast doubt over the future of the Club and it was not until 28th June 1972 that it was finally agreed to make the move to Wong Nai Chung Gap Road. On that red-letter day, the Club's long-serving president, George Rowe, addressed an Extraordinary General Meeting at the Hongkong Club to discuss the future of the HKCC. The 'prophets of doom' had been out in force predicing that the Club would never be the same again if it moved from Chater Road. Apart from the hard core on the General Committee, led by Rowe, secretary Stuart Barnes and grounds convenor Alan Bailey, few were convinced of the positive benefits of the move.

But in the space of less than half an hour, Rowe lifted the gloom as the members present responded enthusiastically to the impressive colour drawings of the architect's plans for the new facilities. It was his stirring speech which finally removed the nagging doubts about the feasibility of such a step and which provided the springboard and impetus for the Club to regain its direction.

"It was a magnificent speech from George which succeeded in bringing around the many doubters and pulling everyone together," recalled Alan Bailey. "He really won the day." Indeed, Rowe's words of wisdom certainly made an impact, with only one of the 235 members in attendance not voting to accept the Government's offer. With such an overwhelming majority agreeing to approve the new building scheme and its inherent financial consequences the wheels were set in motion for the move.

A second EGM was held on 23rd August that year to amend and bring

Site formation in progress at Wong Nai Chung Gap during the early 1970s.

up to date the Articles of Association relating to all categories of membership.

Negotiations with the Government on the terms of removal had been resolved with the Club being offered the following:

(a) An area of approximately 146,000 square feet, which had already been prepared to the extent of levelling and basic drainage.
(b) A recreational lease of 21 years.
(c) A direct grant of HK$75,000 towards the cost of turfing the new ground on condition that the Club continued to maintain the turf at the existing ground to the end of the period of the lease as extended.
(d) In addition, a loan of HK$75,000 towards the cost of further turfing, repayable over ten years at six per cent per annum.

At the same time, a new building scheme for development at Wong Nai Chung Gap was finalised with a total estimated cost of HK$3.8 million. This required a building levy of HK$20 per month in addition to the monthly subscription and also made it necessary for each member to subscribe to a refundable debenture of HK$1,000.

With the backing of the members, the real work began as Alan Bailey and his co-workers commenced the daunting task of organising the digging up of the sacred Chater Road turf and its transportation to the new site. It was almost four months and, with the timing such a crucial factor, work often continued around the clock.

"It was an extremely harrowing experience," recalled Alan Bailey, who took on the huge responsibility of keeping the grass alive as it was transported in 14 lorry loads. The bowling green was the first to be moved followed by the turf from the cricket square and finally the outfield. The blocks of turf, together with 100 tons of peat moss specially shipped in from Ireland, were carefully stored and lovingly treated before being laid down at Wong Nai Chung Gap.

Inevitably there were problems. The bowling green was lifted in

W.V. (Bill) Conway, general manager 1975-88.

Aerial view of the new facilities at Wong Nai Chung Gap.

September 1973 and successfully relaid at the new ground in October. The major disappointment concerned the ground surface at Wong Nai Chung Gap. The seed which was sown on the advice of the Club's English consultants did not grow satisfactorily and the Club was obliged to terminate the services of its ground contractor and take its own measures to deal with the problem. A new contractor was engaged to lift turf from the fringes of the Chater Road ground in June 1974 and this was relaid as the square at the new ground and fortunately took well. In May 1975 at the time of the final move, further turf was removed from Chater Road and placed on the new outfield. It bound sufficiently well during the rainy months to ensure a good playing surface by the start of the season.

Construction work on the new clubhouse.

Meanwhile, the buildings at the new site were well under way. Good progress was being made on the two-storey clubhouse and the manager's flat. Such was the desire to ensure that the facilities were far better than at

Chater Road that the idea of adding a third floor with an additional bar and dining room was mooted. At the AGM in 1974, members gave their authority to go ahead with the extension which meant that the roof of the original building became the Chater Tavern.

Despite difficulties, deadlines were met and the Club was first opened to members on 18th July 1975. The first match, between the Witherers and Nomads, was played on 20th September and the official opening took place on 26th September. On that day, Sir Denys Roberts unveiled two plaques which read: "In commemoration of the transfer of the Hong Kong Cricket Club following one hundred and twenty four years of occupation at Chater Road, Hong Kong, these premises were opened by the president, Sir Denys Roberts, KBE, QC, on September 26, 1975."

"The large crest and lettering erected on the outside wall of the squash courts has been presented by the following companies in appreciation of their close association with the Club and of the facilities granted to their staff over very many years. In addition it was appropriate to present a memorial to the Club to commemorate its move to new premises in the 125th year of its existence. Dodwell & Co Ltd, Hongkong & Shanghai Banking Corporation, Jardine Matheson & Co Ltd, John Swire & Sons Ltd."

Just months before the move took place, Bill Conway, who had been a member for many years, was appointed general manager and was presented with the arduous task of helping the Club to adjust from a central city location to rural

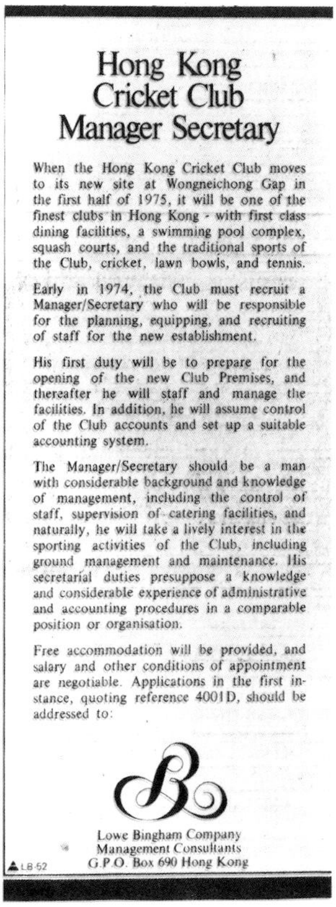

Hong Kong Cricket Club Manager Secretary

When the Hong Kong Cricket Club moves to its new site at Wongneichong Gap in the first half of 1975, it will be one of the finest clubs in Hong Kong - with first class dining facilities, a swimming pool complex, squash courts, and the traditional sports of the Club, cricket, lawn bowls, and tennis.

Early in 1974, the Club must recruit a Manager/Secretary who will be responsible for the planning, equipping, and recruiting of staff for the new establishment.

His first duty will be to prepare for the opening of the new Club Premises, and thereafter he will staff and manage the facilities. In addition, he will assume control of the Club accounts and set up a suitable accounting system.

The Manager/Secretary should be a man with considerable background and knowledge of management, including the control of staff, supervision of catering facilities, and naturally, he will take a lively interest in the sporting activities of the Club, including ground management and maintenance. His secretarial duties presuppose a knowledge and considerable experience of administrative and accounting procedures in a comparable position or organisation.

Free accommodation will be provided, and salary and other conditions of appointment are negotiable. Applications in the first instance, quoting reference 4001D, should be addressed to:

Lowe Bingham Company
Management Consultants
G.P.O. Box 690 Hong Kong

LB 52

Blocks of turf that were transplanted from Chater Road to the new ground at Wong Nai Chung Gap.

surroundings. One immediate consequence was that the Club dining room was no longer strained to capacity at lunchtimes due to the travelling time required to get to and from Wong Nai Chung Gap, although this situation improved when the Aberdeen tunnel opened and made the road from the Club to Central much less congested. On the other hand, whereas four people turning up for dinner at Chater Road constituted a special occasion, now the evening dining period became a most popular time.

Since the move there have been a number of structural changes and modifications, further enhancing the Club's reputation as one of the best in the territory. A staff quarters building, poolside cafeteria, enclosed scorers' room, extended dining room, ground floor bar and car parks have all been added. A floodlit cricket net was installed as well as floodlights for the two tennis courts. Air-conditioning and improved flooring were also provided for the squash courts. The trees and shrubs planted around the field and in the swimming pool area received a severe battering from Typhoon Ellen in 1983, but the ravaged greenery and new plantings flourished.

In the field of administration, the Club changed over to self-accounting in 1976, while in March 1978, another major step forward was taken when it became self-catering. Over the years the Club had always employed contract caterers but this entailed difficulties in quality control. The quality of the food and service now bears no relation to that of the pre-1978 days.

The end of an era came in 1987 when the Club's long-serving president, Sir Denys Roberts, stepped down from office and Bill Conway announced his intention of retiring and returning home to the U.K. Both men contributed greatly to Hong Kong cricket in general and, in particular, both played an enormous role in shaping the recent history of the HKCC. At the Annual General Meeting that year, Mr. Terry Smith, an ex-Captain of Cricket, was elected as president and a few months later the committee announced the appointment of Mr. Keith Garner as the new general manager, with effect from 1st August 1988. ■

(Overleaf) Panoramic view of Central district in the late 19th century.

LEAGUE CRICKET

Although cricket in Hong Kong is believed to have started in 1846, it was not until more than half a century later that a league was formed. With a shield being donated by the South China Morning Post newspaper, a league competition got under way in late 1903 with eight teams taking part.

However, numerous people were outspoken in their opposition to the formation of an organised league. Several critics described the set up as "second class" although the Hong Kong Weekly Press was quick to point out the term "did not imply social distinction". Nevertheless, the league flourished with the Army Ordinance Corps having the distinction of being crowned the first Hong Kong cricket champions.

A combination of positive media coverage plus an ever-growing influx of expatriates brought added interest with new teams keen to get involved. In 1904, the Kowloon Cricket Club (KCC) joined and three years later was followed by the Eastern Extension Telegraph Company. The other major force in those early days was Craigengower Cricket Club, who along with KCC won the title twice before the HKCC joined the roll of honour.

Surprisingly it was the 'B' team which made the breakthrough in 1908-09, although the strength of that side was said to be on a par with the 'A' team. Even then the rivalry between HKCC teams, which has been carried on to this day, was evident, and the 'A' team landed the First Division championship 12 months later.

At that stage the mainstays of the league were HKCC, the Police, KCC, Hong Kong University, Craigengower and the Indian Recreation Club. Almost 80 years on, all those clubs are still in existence — although not all are playing at the same grounds — and playing an active role in cricket in the territory.

One of the game's staunchest supporters was Sir Henry May, the Governor of Hong Kong from 1912 to 1919. His enthusiasm was shared by the Colonial Secretary, Claude Severn, and May's private secretary, Ponsonby Fane. The stories of Fane's exploits are legendary. Turning out for Hong Kong University, his eccentric habits (he

Duncan Kilgour, popular captain of Hong Kong Cricket Club Witherers in the 1980s.

batted and kept wicket without pads and apparently never took a bath) became one of the main talking points in cricketing circles.

The HKCC 'B' team were successful again in 1912-13 after which the Club decided to pool its resources into one side playing under the banner of the Hong Kong Cricket Club. In their first season they asserted their authority by taking the title before a three-year suspension of the league due to World War I.

When the league resumed in 1917-18, the HKCC, with predominantly the same players, made a successful defence of their championship. Despite that triumph, reports indicate that the Club opted out of league cricket the following year (it did so again for one season towards the end of the 1920s) playing only friendlies.

With more Services venues becoming available and the game continuing to grow in popularity, it was decided to form a Second Division in 1921. As well as offering more people the opportunity to turn out at weekends, the Second Division also allowed the primarily social players to perform among themselves at a lower level than the top flight.

Between 1921 and 1941 cricket thrived in the territory with the HKCC winning the First Division outright on four occasions (1923-24, 1928-29, 1933-34 and 1934-35) and earning a joint share with the Indian Recreation Club in 1936-37. The Second Division team also enjoyed plenty of success, particularly in the late 1920s when they finished on top of the standings two years in a row.

Organised cricket came to an abrupt halt in 1941, but fears that the

Benny Kwong Wo, talented all-round cricketer and lawn bowler, now the Club's head groundsman.

game would never regain its popularity were allayed after Admiral Harcourt's task force had taken the Japanese surrender in 1945. Much work was required at the majority of the grounds to restore them to their pre-war conditions after being taken over for a variety of uses. The Navy had taken over the Chater Road ground, while Kowloon Cricket Club was rescued from the grazing of the Japanese mules.

The leagues resumed in 1948 under the same format with a number of new teams, and Optimists and Scorpions replacing the 'A' and 'B' teams at the HKCC. Their formation helped swell the First Division to 10 teams with each side playing against their nine opponents on a home-and-away basis, giving an 18-game programme. The scoring system in those days could not have been more straightforward. The winning team was awarded four points, with none to the losers. A draw resulted in each team claiming one point.

Scorpions, under the leadership of the Club captain Alec Pearce, showed from the first post-war season that they were a force to be reckoned with. They finished as runners-up, winning 11 and losing four matches. Three of the reversals were by narrow margins — by one wicket against Hong Kong University and by 14 and 27 runs to eventual champions Club de Recreio.

Talented all-round sportsman Leonard Stokes, who starred for Shanghai Cricket Club pre-war, was the linchpin of the batting. The aggressive and immensely strong opener compiled 613 runs in 17 visits to the crease at an impressive average of 55.73. The spearhead of the bowling attack was off-spinner Frank Howarth, who to this day remains the most prolific wicket-taker in the history of league cricket in Hong Kong. Coming in off less than half a dozen paces, Howarth, who had played as a professional in the Lancashire League before the war, picked up 53 wickets at 10.91 each.

Pearce, the eldest son of former HKCC captain Tam Pearce, had

1974. Wanderers' captain Mike Duggan with the Rothmans Cup.

previously represented Kent in the English County Championship and he featured in some of the highlights of the season. He shared an opening stand of 172 with Stokes in a drawn match with clubmates Optimists and took eight wickets for 31 with his off-cutters in the drawn encounter at KCC's Cox's Road ground.

The promise shown in 1948-49 was fulfilled the following season when Scorpions stormed to the title, winning 15 games and losing just once, by one wicket in a thrilling game with Army. Stokes and Howarth were again very much to the fore. Stokes, who had shown what a good eye he had when playing baseball for the British team during his imprisonment in Shanghai, hit two half-centuries and a brilliant 118 against the Third Commando Brigade.

With versatile youngster Tony Weller, Otto Kerr and Pearce also scoring more than 250 runs each, Scorpions were especially adept at chasing. The bowling was dominated by Howarth, by now in his 40s. He delivered 311 overs and captured a staggering 103 wickets — a record which is never likely to be surpassed. Bemusing batsmen with his flight and subtle variation of pace, Howarth claimed five or more wickets in an innings on no fewer than 13 occasions. For the second season in succession he performed the hat trick, while his most astonishing effort came against Craigengower when he destroyed the home team with a return of nine for 26.

In 1950-51, with Stokes unable to reproduce his previous season's form with the bat and Howarth playing just a handful of matches, Scorpions failed to repeat the 1949-50 success and had to be content with sharing the runners-up spot with Optimists. Despite bowling only 71.2 overs, Howarth still managed to pick up 31 wickets at a cost of 6.06 each to top the bowling averages. Again he turned in the outstanding individual performance of the season when he took nine for 11 against Recreio.

Laurie Kilbee celebrated his final season in charge of Optimists with numerous reliable innings and by guiding them to their best-ever finish and, perhaps more importantly, their first victory against Scorpions — a tense two-wicket triumph. Kilbee served the Club for several years and his two sons, John and Chris, both developed into excellent players. John captained a Club Cricket Conference team on an overseas tour, while Chris represented Singapore in the 1987 Interport against Hong Kong.

In West Australian Noel Arthy, Optimists possessed one of the most accomplished opening batsmen in the Club's history. He has the distinction of being the only HKCC player to have topped the batting averages for three years in a row — 1949-50 to 1951-52 inclusive. Another outstanding Optimist of that era was Rory Macpherson, an aggressive batsman who invariably made quick runs and a superbly athletic fielder who also excelled at tennis and squash.

Following a couple of disappointing seasons, Scorpions and Optimists were involved in a two-horse battle for the 1952-53 title with the former eventually scraping home by three points to record their second championship win. Ivor Stanton, a chartered surveyor, provided the steadying influence to the Scorpions' batting which had been missing since their previous success. The tall, methodical opener made 696 runs including two centuries, while Pearce chipped in with a crucial match-winning ton against Hong Kong University.

Harry Owen-Hughes, whose association with the Club dated back to the late 1920s, and Donald Leach, a former captain of Shanghai, complemented useful displays with the bat by also securing some vital wickets. Owen-Hughes, a Lieutenant-Colonel, was a die-hard Scorpion who continued to play regularly almost up to his 60th birthday. He occasionally stood in as an emergency wicket-keeper who insisted on using only a right hand glove and keeping his left hand free.

Others who contributed to the 1952-53 triumph included opening bowler Chris Connett and that man Howarth, who despite making just five appearances still managed to head the bowling charts. Swing bowler Ian Herridge also turned in some decisive spells, but in spite of Scorpions'

(Top right) HKCC Nomads, 2nd Division Champions 1968-69.
(Bottom right) HKCC Witherers, Saturday League Runners-up and Gillette Cup Winners 1984-85.

success, signs began to emerge that Optimists were almost ready to take over the mantle as the HKCC's top team.

With Guy Pritchard, another man of Kent, proving an astute leader and a clever bowler in the first of his 11 successive seasons at the helm, Optimists at last began to shake off the hold Scorpions had had over them. However, success did not come immediately. Scorpions narrowly failed to retain their title in 1953-54 finishing runners-up to Army with Optimists two points further adrift in third place.

Inconsistent batting was the downfall for Optimists whose bowlers performed admirably. Ken Spink, a medium-pacer who cut the ball off the wicket, had six hauls of five wickets or more while burly Australian Tommy Mahon took seven for eight with his booming outswingers against Recreio. Mahon — the Government chemist — also provided one of the highlights of a disappointing 1954-55 season when he took six for 50 to dismiss Scorpions cheaply in the derby match. John Leader, a marvellous timer of the ball, with 89 not out and left-hander Pritchard with an unbeaten 54 then put on an undefeated 143 for the first wicket to give Optimists a memorable 10-wicket triumph.

Despite the consistency with the bat of Tony Weller, who had distinguished

HONG KONG

OPTIMISTS v SCORPION

Kwong Wo H.W. Paterson I.L.J. Stevens C. Corder E.C. Cannon I.L. Stanton

P.H. Davies J.C.G. Murphy W.E.G. Williams (Optimists Capt.) G.T. Rowe (President)

R.M. Evan Jones

RICKET CLUB

– 13TH JANUARY 1968

angston M.J. Miles M. Duggan G.H.P. Pritchard R.W. Barker R.H. Mills-Owen

E.H. Wilson (Club Capt.) J.K. Fawcett (Scorpions Capt.) J.F. Muirhead F.A. Weller

M.R.V. Clinch

himself as an outstanding soccer player, Scorpions failed to impress in 1955-56. While Optimists finished the 1956-57 campaign as runners-up to Army South and KCC, Scorpions experienced their worst-ever season, winning just three of their 20 games. Pritchard, Leader, slow left-armer Mike Watts and Mahon all displayed good form for Optimists, while wicket-keeper Ray Hughes was rewarded for his reliable performances with 30 victims, of which no fewer than 17 were stumpings.

The resurgence of Scorpions in 1957-58 principally came about as a result of Howarth's decision to come out of retirement. It was the first time since 1949-50 that he had bowled more than 100 overs in a season and he showed he had lost none of the guile or accuracy which had served him so well in his heyday. Howarth finished the campaign with 58 wickets at 14.09 apiece and found an excellent ally in on-the-spot medium-pacer Len White — one of the few players to have represented both Scorpions and Optimists for a full season.

Even more surprising than Scorpions' revival was the lacklustre effort of the Optimists for whom the only player to emerge with an impressive record was wicket-keeper Hughes. In 15 matches, the superintendent for Crown Lands was involved in 23 dismissals. Seventeen were stumpings — mostly off Pritchard — with no fewer than six coming in one game against Recreio.

After six seasons in the trophy wilderness, the tide again turned for the Club in 1959-60 with Optimists at last winning their first championship. With captain Pritchard providing the backbone in both batting and bowling, Optimists shrugged off the many disappointments of the previous decade by winning 10 of their 18 games and losing just three — ironically, two of those were against Scorpions who experienced a miserable season and finished well down the table.

In true captain's style, Pritchard led from the front, scoring 490 runs and topping the bowling averages with his mixture of swing and spin with 40 wickets at 10.72 as well as finishing as the leading fielder with eight outfield catches. Among Pritchard's victims were a couple who were deceived by

Bob Fotheringham, left arm pace bowler who also represented Hong Kong.

his change to bowling underarm — a ploy he often adopted in a bid to achieve a breakthrough.

On one occasion in the late 1960s, Pritchard resorted to underarm to try and dislodge a particularly obdurate Kowloon Cricket Club batsman who had occupied the crease for a lengthy spell and seemed intent on boring Optimists into submission. Having watched other bowlers toil away unsuccessfully all afternoon, Pritchard came into the attack bowling underarm. And justifying the move he trapped the batsman 'leg before' second ball and Optimists went on to win.

The 1959-60 triumph of Optimists was, however, by no means a one-man effort. In addition to Pritchard, John Leader and George Rowe, a stylish strokemaker, amassed more than 350 runs while Ken Spink, slow left-armer Gordon Williams and young off-spinner Mike Duggan all claimed in excess of 25 wickets. Strangely, the majority of the Club's best individual efforts that season came from Scorpions players. They had the top three in the batting averages, led by left-handed Australian opener Dean Barrett with 660 runs at more than 50. But unlike their sister side, Scorpions were unable to bowl out their opposition.

The Optimists' team spirit was illustrated in a pre-Christmas encounter with Recreio. Chasing a not particularly substantial total, Optimists lost their first seven wickets cheaply and appeared to be sliding to an inglorious defeat. But late middle-order batsmen Spink and Major Clive Ship, who was to become the first captain of the Wanderers, compiled an unbroken eighth-wicket partnership of 63 to see their side home.

The first tamperings with the points system came in 1960-61 with the award of bonus points in a drawn match. Two points were awarded for the 'winning draw' and one for the 'losing draw.' With Gordon Williams taking advantage of the fact that the Chater Road wicket again favoured bowlers (he claimed 61 wickets — all four of his five-wicket returns coming on home ground), Optimists had another good season and narrowly failed to retain the title which was won by Army Brigade.

In 1961-62, Barrett, who was to

become managing director of China Light and Power, surpassed 500 runs for the third season in succession but Scorpions continued to fall from grace finishing seventh in the 11-team league. Optimists ended fourth with Pritchard again making an outstanding contribution with 580 runs and 31 wickets.

With John Baker taking over the captaincy from Pritchard, Optimists won their second title in five years in 1963-64, pipping second-placed Scorpions by four points. In his second season with the team, Peter 'Dad' Langston provided the key thrust with a host of match-winning performances with the ball. Thundering in from the Murray Road car park end off his long run with his shirt hanging out, Langston unsettled many batsmen with his deceptive late movement.

His 61 wickets that season cost just 8.11 apiece and included some remarkable spells — most notably an 11.1 over stint which brought him seven wickets for five runs against Recreio. Despite having stood down as skipper, Pritchard was still a major influence with both bat and ball. He featured in an unbroken century stand with Rowe (whose son Charles turned out occasionally when back on school holidays and went on to represent Kent and Glamorgan in the County Championship) in a sweet nine-wicket thrashing of Scorpions.

John 'Foxy' Fawcett, in only his second year with the Club, showed indications of being an instrumental player for Scorpions. Particularly punishing off the back foot and on the leg side the left-hander was top of the 1964-65 batting averages, including a magnificent unbeaten century in a drawn match with champions Army. With both teams still in the process of rebuilding, 1965-66 — when further changes to the points system were

Alan Telford from New Zealand. One of the fastest bowlers to represent the HKCC during the 1980s.

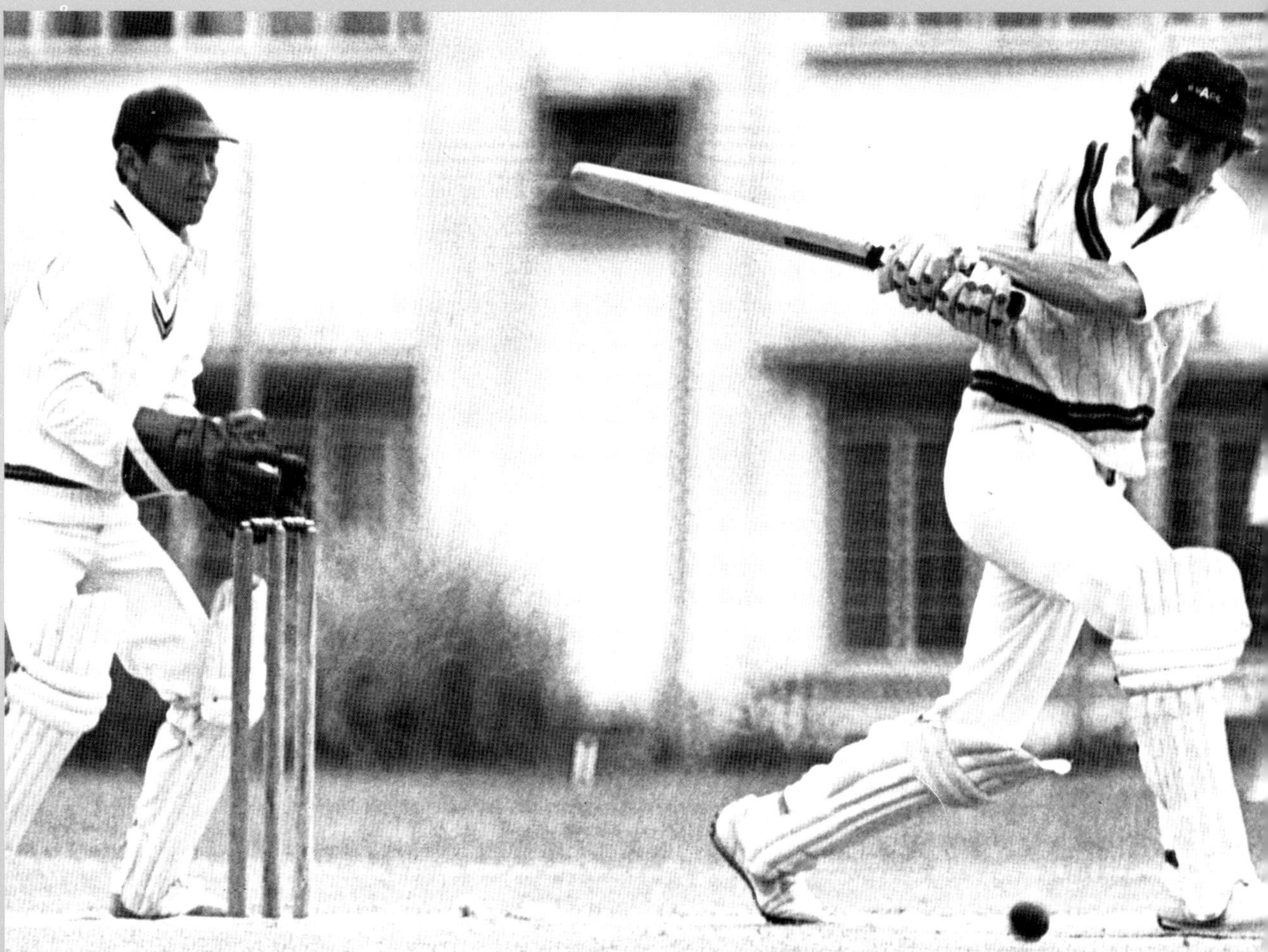

Rod Eddington, Australian all-rounder and
Captain of Cricket during the 1980s.

introduced — proved a season of transition.

But Scorpions, under the leadership of Ted Wilson, recovered quickly and swept all before them to capture the 1966-67 title — their first for 14 seasons — in convincing style. Recording outright victories in 15 of their 20 matches, many of them by huge margins, they proved far too strong for all their rivals. Fawcett, generally going in at the fall of the first wicket, was a model of consistency amassing 541 runs at an average of more than 54.

On the batting front there was plenty of depth with Tony Weller still plundering runs regularly despite nervous beginnings, and lanky Julian Murphy, Judge Noel Hooper and Ivor Stanton also chipping in. Bowling-wise, right-arm paceman Fawcett and fellow-opener Murphy were the chief destroyers, between them claiming 114 wickets. Medium-pacer Wilson, who went on to become president of the Hong Kong Cricket Association and now represents Hong Kong on the Test and County Cricket Board, and slow left-armer Hamish Muirhead both offered worthy back-up.

With Wilson, who had previously skippered East Africa, taking over as Captain of Cricket, Fawcett stepped into the breach for Scorpions and successfully emulated his predecessor by leading his side to the retention of their crown. Again it was an overwhelming triumph as they finished 42 points clear of Optimists, who with new young batsman Peter Davies making a big impression took the runners-up spot.

The pressures of captaincy did nothing to detract from the form of Fawcett whose potent double act with Murphy was once again a decisive factor. Although the Scorpions' monopoly was broken the following year, the outlook continued to appear bright for the Club with promising young players coming through, while numbers were also boosted by the 'signing up' of quality players who came to the territory.

Such was the popularity of cricket towards the end of the 1960s that the HKCA felt compelled to take a long, hard look at the set up. One of the innovations to try and improve standards was the formation of a Super League on Sundays. The league consisted of four teams — HKCC, Combined Services, Kowloon (comprising KCC and Recreio players) and Valley (made up of the cream of Police, Indian Recreation Club, Little Sai Wan and Craigengower), who won the competition.

Although that did not last, further changes were brought about in 1969-70 in an attempt to give players of all ability a fair crack of the whip. The First Division was switched from its traditional Saturday afternoon slot to all-day games on Sundays in the belief that it would provide more competitive cricket for the top players and prepare them better for the Interports and overseas tours. The Second Division was to continue on Saturday afternoons. However, with people generally unprepared or unable to devote their Sundays to cricket, fewer Sunday teams were entered into the league and the Second Division became the stronger of the two.

While Nomads, who were still very much in their infancy, won the Second Division two years on the trot, Optimists returned to their former glories by taking the First Division title in 1971-72. Peter Davies, who was earning a reputation as the territory's most prolific run-scorer, led the way with 674 runs while John Ashworth was the pick of the bowlers.

Realising that the new structure was not working out as planned, the HKCA again changed the format at the end of the 1972-73 campaign. This time the divisions were restructured to provide for separate Saturday and Sunday leagues — a move which proved more acceptable to everyone and remained in operation upto the end of the 1986-87 season, when due to the exodus of expatriates a Super League was reintroduced.

The first season of the revamped leagues saw the HKCC field three Sunday teams — Optimists, Scorpions

Peter Olsen, a fine wicket-keeper, forcing batsman and comedian.

and Wanderers — and two Saturday sides, Nomads and Witherers. For several years, Wanderers, with Stuart Barnes at the helm, had been a social side who played friendlies every Sunday and who went on exotic tours. They stepped into the league at the last minute to make up the numbers and did not take long to bridge the gap with their sister sides.

It turned out to be a memorable season for the Club. Optimists, with Davies narrowly missing out on 1,000 runs, were runners-up to KCC Templars with Wanderers, inspired by the pace bowling of Dave Wellard, coming third. Led by Mike Duggan, Wanderers became the first HKCC team to win the limited overs Rothmans Cup since its inception in 1970-71. Another piece of silverware was added to the sideboard when Nomads swept to the Saturday title, losing just one of their 26 matches. Witherers finished 40 points adrift in second place.

The stars of the Nomads' triumph were Mark Tress, scorer of three centuries and with an average of 74.50, Peter Green (the first Hong Kong player to make a hundred on an international tour) and Duggan. Meanwhile, Davies, by now an automatic choice for any Hong Kong team, was recognised for his efforts by being named the Ruttonjee Player of the Year — the highest accolade for an individual in Hong Kong cricket.

The achievements of 1973-74 were a hard act to follow and the HKCC was unable to complete its final historic season at Chater Road by capturing a trophy. With the impending move to Wong Nai Chung Gap it was a season tinged with much sadness. The last century in a league match at Chater Road was made by Sir Edwin Bramall, who hit an unbeaten 112 for the Army against Witherers on March 15, 1975.

With off-field activities tending to take priority in the first season at their new home, the performances of the teams were not particularly impressive. However, the wheel of fortune turned slightly in the HKCC's favour in 1976-77 with the Rothmans Cup victory of Optimists signalling the dawning of one of the greatest eras in the Club's history. Over the next eight seasons, HKCC teams were to capture a total of 15 major trophies — five Sunday Leagues, four Saturday

Leagues, five Gillette Cups and one Rothmans Cup.

Skippered by slow bowler Bob Toes, a youthful Wanderers side set the ball rolling by becoming the Club's first Sunday League champions in 1977-78. Elegant left-hander Martin Sabine was the linchpin of the batting while Toes shared the bowling responsibilities with paceman Terry Smith and Mike Duggan, a great servant to the Club and a spin bowler with superb flight.

Left-handed Hong Kong opener Graham Turner made numerous significant contributions with the bat to lead Nomads — unquestionably the Club's most successful team over the past decade — to the Saturday League title. However, over the next two years it was Optimists who sprang to the forefront of attention with successive Sunday League triumphs.

Benefitting from the seasoned experience of their players under the shrewd guidance of John Ashworth, Optimists gelled into a formidable team. In addition to the natural talent and ability of the side, one of their greatest attributes was their determination and refusal to bow under pressure, resulting in their going through the 1978-79 season undefeated and losing only twice the following year. In a dramatic culmination to the 1979-80 campaign, Optimists' chances of retaining the title hung very much in the balance.

Entertaining Vagabonds, who held a one-point lead over them at the start of the final round of matches, Optimists needed victory to ensure KCC Infidels would not be able to pip them. Thanks to a gutsy eighth-wicket stand of 48 between Ashcroft and Jim Hughes, Optimists were able to reach the relative respectability of 182. Ashworth and left-armer Martin Lewis then got to work and reduced Vagabonds to 170 for eight with two overs remaining. In an amazing finale, a run out was followed by Ashworth claiming the final wicket to leave his side victors by 12 runs.

It was fitting that it should have been Ashworth who delivered the telling final contribution. It completed his 10th season with Optimists, seven of which he had been captain, during which time he did not miss a single match. Another key man for Optimists

Geoff Foster (wicket-keeper) and James Barrington, who both represented the HKCC and Hong Kong with distinction.

was big-hearted medium-pacer Steve Willis who departed Hong Kong before the second successive championship had been sealed.

The 1980-81 season was memorable for the fact that Nomads completed an unprecedented hat trick of Saturday League Cup victories, the last two under the sponsorship of Gillette. In a tense, low-scoring final they beat the star-studded King George V School team by two wickets with Paul Dunnett striking the winning runs from the last ball of the match.

Pepped by a trio of talented Australians, Scorpions ended a 14-year drought when they won the 1981-82 Sunday League championship. David Clarke, a fine all-rounder, forceful opening batsman John Hollioake and solid left-hander Rod Eddington — who won a share of the Player of the Year trophy — all played major roles and were rewarded by earning representative honours. However, it was a fine team effort with Dennis Way forging a formidable new-ball partnership with Clarke, and Chinese all-rounder Benny Kwong-wo rediscovering his confidence with bat and ball after several seasons in the doldrums.

The 1982-83 campaign was notable for the formation of a third HKCC Saturday League team, Gap Ramblers, and the return to trophy-winning ways of Nomads and Wanderers. Nomads won their third Saturday League crown, but for them it was only the start of a glorious three-year spell, while Wanderers won their second Rothmans title by beating Scorpions in what to date has been the only all-HKCC final.

The three-pronged attack of Bob Fotheringham, Neil Smith and Kwong-wo guided Scorpions to the 1983-84 title — their second Sunday League triumph in three years. Between them, left-armer Fotheringham, the broad-shouldered Smith and Kwong-wo, who showed superb variety with his cunning mix of leg-breaks, googlies and off-spin, took no fewer than 120 of

HKCC Wanderers, Sunday League and Rothmans Cup Winners 1987-88.

Two master batsmen from different eras: R. Ponsonby Fane (left) and the "Great Man" Peter H. Davies.

the 135 wickets claimed by the team.

With Paul Varty leading by example, Scorpions won their final two matches thanks to some gutsy middle-order recoveries to enable them to oust longtime leaders Optimists at the death. For the first time the three HKCC teams filled the top three positions. Nomads, meanwhile, created history by retaining the Saturday title and becoming the first team to achieve the League and Gillette Cup double. And there was more to come as David Sibree's side completed a unique treble by taking the 1984-85 title.

Fielding virtually the same team as the previous season, they made clubmates Witherers pay for a crucial slip in the penultimate game of the campaign. Talented young Queenslander Paul Veivers was the outstanding batsman. The bowling was spearheaded by left-armers Fotheringham and Nick Tonkinson. Witherers gained some consolation for their failure to halt Nomads' run by winning the Gillette Cup — their first trophy.

Since then, the continuing departure of players from Hong Kong coupled with the lack of new blood and the problems of availability have combined to dent the HKCC's chances of adding to their already impressive list of successes.

Indeed, over the past couple of years of the Club has lost the services of many outstanding talents. Among them are Peter Davies, Peter 'Plod' Anderson, whose tactical astuteness and leadership qualities, coupled with his batting skills, saw him captain the national team with distinction for two mini World Cup campaigns and Oxbridge batsman James Barrington. Australian all-rounder Brad Jones and New Zealand paceman Alan Telford, both of whom made a big impression during their brief stints in the territory, have also moved on.

Of the 'old school', only Martin Sabine, Bob Fotheringham and Peter Olsen — arguably the best wicket-keeper the Club has ever had — remain. Nevertheless, history has proved that the HKCC always bounce back from adversity and it's a safe bet that it won't be too long before the honours start rolling in again. ■

(Overleaf) View from the Peak showing the Chater Road ground with the first pavilion in the late 1880s.

INTERPORTS

The Shanghai Years (1866 — 1948)

According to the Wisden Anthology (1963-1982), "It was warm and sunny in Melbourne on March 15, 1877 when Australia's Charles Bannerman took guard and prepared to receive the first ball from Alfred Shaw of England in what has come to be universally regarded as the first Test match."

What is not quite so well known is that more than 10 years prior to the pioneering tour of James Lilywhite's team, Hong Kong were involved in one of cricket's first international matches. Despite problems with transport, it was in February 1866 that the inaugural Hong Kong-Shanghai Interport was played.

The venue was the Hong Kong Cricket Club's Chater Road ground, and for those early challenges the Hong Kong team was selected by and comprised almost exclusively of HKCC members. The HKCC and its Shanghai Cricket Club counterparts continued to be the main driving force behind the contests, though military players strengthened both teams, and Hong Kong in particular were later able to call upon members of other clubs.

Nevertheless, the Chater Road ground remained the venue for Hong Kong home matches. It is difficult to imagine what conditions were like in those early days, but in any case the Interport series thrived and was an important social and sporting fixture in both outposts of the empire on the China coastline.

The 82-year history of the series, during which time the teams did battle on 38 occasions, was marked by many remarkable characters and some outstanding cricket and cricketers. However, the most lasting memory will sadly be of the 1892 tragedy when the lives of 11 of the Hong Kong team were lost in the sinking of the ill-fated SS Bokhara on the return journey from Shanghai.

Although the disaster cast an immovable shadow over the series, the deep sense of loss felt on both sides brought about a camaraderie which enabled it to continue and survive two world wars. It was not until late 1948, when Shanghai became embroiled in the bitter fighting of civil war that the

(Facing page top) 1912. Hong Kong and Shanghai teams for the Interport fixture.

SHANGHAI V. HONG KONG IN HONG KONG, 1912

Third row :— P. M. Hodgson (*Hon. Secretary*), A. A. Claxton, Lamb, Capt. Crawford, R.G.A., Lt. Bagnall, R.G.A., A. E. Lanning, H. B. Ollerdessen, Tait.

Second row :— Cpl. Dempsey, G. R. Sayer, Lt. White, R. O. Hutchison, McEwen, W. J. Haynes, Lt. Christian, R.G.A., H. E. Muriel.

Front row :— J. A. Quayle, R. N. Anderson, W. C. D. Turner, L. Walker (*Capt. Shanghai*), H.E. The Governor, Sir Henry May, H. R. B. Hancock (*Capt. H.K.*), F. Maitland (*President*), V. H. Lanning, A. C. E. Elborough, L. H. W. Crockwell.

HONG KONG TEAM VISITING SHANGHAI 1891

Back row :— Lt. Young, C. S. Barff, Newton, F. Maitland, L. Barff, Capt. Loring.

Front row :—Major Hannay, E. A. Ram, E. W. Maitland, Capt. Dumbleton, Capt. Dunn, Lt. Boyle, Dr. Lowson.

HONG KONG CRICKET LEAGUE V MALAYSIAN CRICKET ASSOCIATION

IN HONG KONG – NOVEMBER 1963 – WON BY HONG KONG

HONG KONG C. L. XI

HONG KONG C. L. XI

Back Row: L to R

G. A. LEMAY (Scorer) M. MELLOWS (Ump.) R. LALCHANDANI J. DYBALL (12th man) P. HALL
G. ABBASS J. HALL J. FAWCETT E. dos. REMEDIOS CAPT. HENDERSON (Ump.)

Front Row: L to R

C. MYATT F. A. WELLER D. G. COFFEY (Capt.) B. P. DHABER J. SHROFF

1963. Hong Kong League XI vs Malaysian Cricket Association.

INTERPORT
HONG KONG v SINGAPORE

HONG KONG 7, 8, 9 NOVEMBER 1969
WON BY HONG KONG BY 5 WICKETS

STANDING

Mr. F. Apps B. Kwong E. Silva (Scorer) A. Lewis P. Davies K. Moorthy R. Spalding P. Remedios (Vice President) S. Sivalingam P. Mitchell
S. Kasinathan M. Duggan M. Lloyd D. Dalrymple G. Stokes (Scorer) Mr. W. Hampton

SEATED

J. Jeremiah H. Ebrahim R. Stevens C. Myatt R. da Silva J. Shroff J. Martens R. Lalchandani R. Tessensohn I. Lacy-Smith G. Jarman

1969. Hong Kong and Singapore XIs in front of the Chater Road pavilion.

historical cricketing link was forceably broken.

Even though the majority of those who played an active role in the matches are no longer with us, many unforgettable memories — in the greatest cricketing tradition — have been handed down through the generations and live on to this day.

Can any other series claim an instance of a 'Russian empress' being forced to arrange her travel plans around a cricket match? Or a game decided by a six-hit which was recovered more than a mile from the ground? Or the legendary singing of a player who was described as "having no strokes and a firm voice"?

The first tale concerns prolific Hong Kong batsman Tam Pearce, who played his first Interport in 1903 and continued to be a mainstay until his final appearance in 1935. When Hong Kong visited Shanghai in May 1923, Pearce had reportedly arranged to travel home via Canada on the ship 'The Empress of Russia' at the end of the match.

Putting the imminent departure of 'The Empress of Russia' to the back of his mind, Pearce dug himself in. When the winning hit was made with three wickets still intact just prior to tea on the fourth day, Pearce was still there with 145 runs to his name.

With Hong Kong apparently heading for a heavy defeat, the match seemed likely to end on the third day. Set what was considered an impossible task of scoring more than 270 in the fourth innings, Hong Kong lost an early wicket to leave their hopes resting squarely on Pearce's shoulders.

Mixing watchful defence with punishing drives and cuts off the loose deliveries, Pearce defied everything the Shanghai bowlers threw at him in a memorable innings which threatened to jeopardize his trip. However the officials on 'The Empress of Russia' obviously realised the importance of Pearce's Shanghai mission and are reported to have sportingly postponed her departure until the conclusion of the match.

The previous year's encounter at Chater Road had very much belonged to Shanghai skipper G.M. Billings who almost single-handedly led his team to

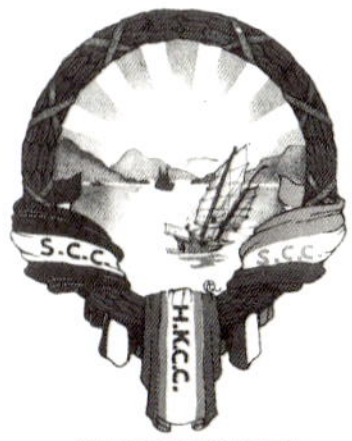

INTERPORT
NOV.-CRICKET-1924
MALAYA
SHANGHAI
HONGKONG

an unlikely triumph in a stunning climax to a game which Hong Kong had for the most part dominated.

Needing 200 for victory, by far the biggest score of the match, Donald Leach put the visitors in contention with a sparkling 79. Upon his dismissal the pendulum appeared to have swung back in Hong Kong's favour, but Billings, who had made 38 out of Shanghai's first innings of 86 after coming in at number 10, had other ideas.

Again coming to the crease at the fall of the eighth wicket, Billings took the bull by the horns, edging his side towards their target before ending the contest with a towering six which landed in a passing tram. The ball was eventually recovered from Central Market. In addition to his heroic batting exploits, Billings had been the chief Hong Kong destroyer, capturing eight wickets.

The forging of friendships became synonymous with the series. With so many extrovert characters, the regular and varied off-the-field entertainment became as much a part of the proceedings as the game itself. And E.G. Barnes, the Shanghai wicket-keeper during the mid-'20s, was one of those who made more of a name for himself in the clubhouse than on the field.

Renowned as a dogged number 11 batsman. Barnes provided hours of good-humoured fun for team-mates and opponents alike. The HKCC's centenary handbook recalled: "Barney had a delightful falsetto voice and many will remember with pleasure the duet, an adaptation of the 'Keys of Heaven', which he used to sing with Donald Leach. Donald sang a good length baritone, coming in slightly from the off tonsil."

One of the features of the matches over the years was the contributions of some supremely talented cricketers. Few made as big an impression as the deadly Shanghai duo consisting of Ivo Barrett and Dr. D.W.E. O'Hara. Barrett, who was briefly to distinguish himself in the English County Championship, made his Interport debut in 1914 and wasted no time in illustrating his immense ability. He cracked an even hundred in the first innings and added a stylish 43 in his second visit to the

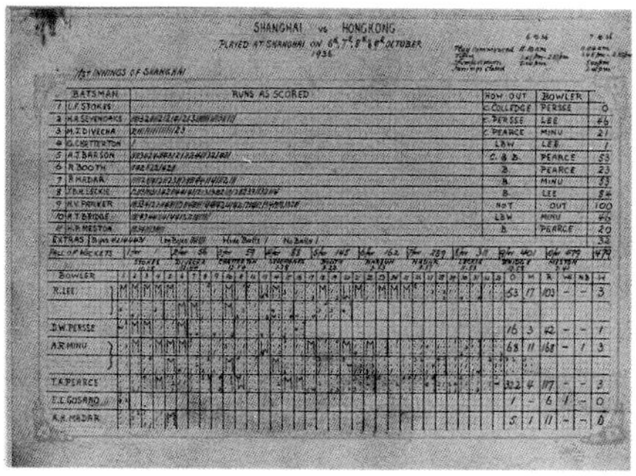
SHANGHAI vs HONGKONG

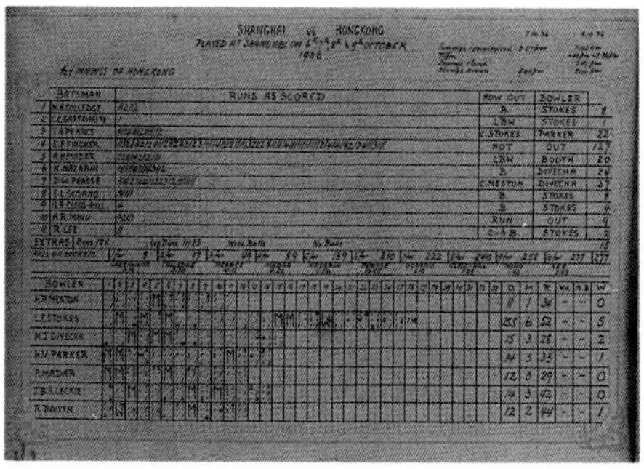
SHANGHAI vs HONGKONG

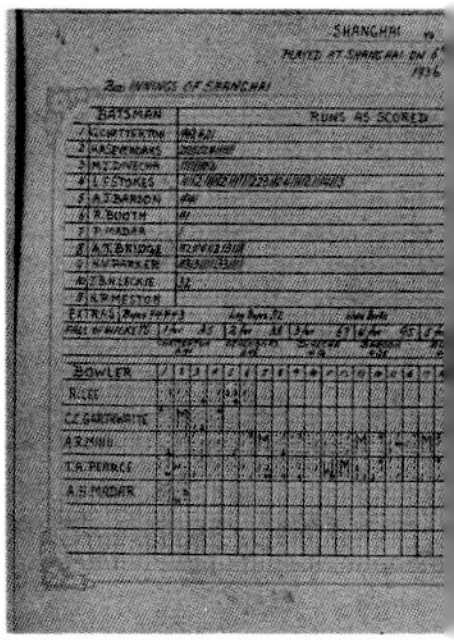

(*Left*) 1929. Hong Kong team vs Shanghai.
(*Bottom*) 1947. A moment's silence prior to the first post-war Interport against Shanghai.

crease to take his side to a comprehensive triumph on home soil. When the series resumed six years later, Barrett's absence was sorely missed by Shanghai, who went down by six wickets.

While Shanghai were struggling, Captain Barrett was making a name for himself in England. In addition to compiling numerous big scores for Hampshire, Barrett excelled for the Gentlemen against the Players and finished the English season near the top of the first-class batting averages.

However, it was only a temporary reprieve for the Hong Kong bowlers, who had to contend with Barrett again in 1921. And it could hardly have been a more spectacular return as Barrett plundered a magnificent 165 — the highest individual score of the entire series — to set up a crushing Shanghai victory by an innings and 159 runs.

With Barrett having deflated the spirits of a weak Hong Kong side, Dr. O'Hara got to work. O'Hara, who had played Grade cricket in Australia and by all accounts might well have risen to the full Test team had he remained there, marked his first Interport appearance with a devastating display of left-arm bowling which saw him claim a match haul of 13 wickets for 88 runs.

The individual performances of Barrett and O'Hara continued to dominate the matches for several years. O'Hara took 11 wickets in Shanghai's 1926 success while Barrett, who retired to England in 1928, produced arguably his finest innings in 1927 on a Chater Road strip described as being "distinctly temperamental". While his colleagues struggled for survival, Barrett called on all his technical skill and mastery to stand firm in an innings of 146 made from the all out Shanghai total of 260. However, despite that effort Hong Kong scraped home by three wickets thanks to another gutsy knock from Tam Pearce and some solid blows from W. Brace, who proved an exceptional all-rounder in his brief term in the territory.

While the departure of Barrett left a major void in the Shanghai side, Hong

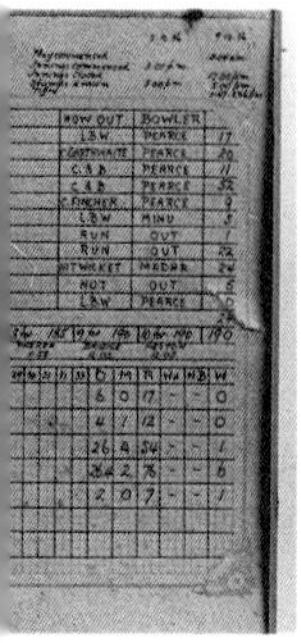

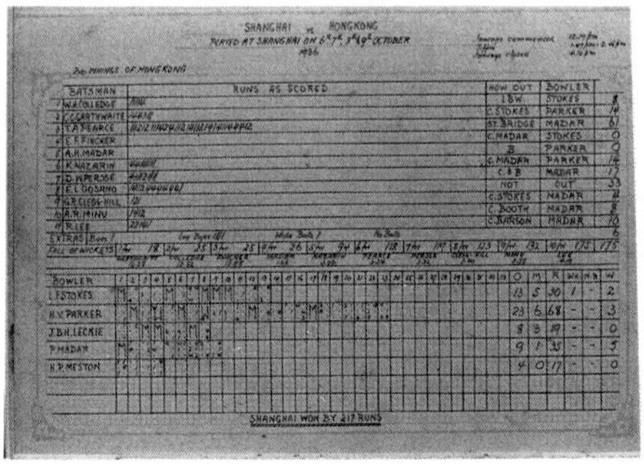

SHANGHAI vs HONGKONG
PLAYED AT SHANGHAI ON 6th 7th 8th & 9th OCTOBER 1936

2nd INNINGS OF HONGKONG

	Batsman	How out	Bowler	
1	W.H.COLLEDGE	L.B.W.	STOKES	8
2	C.C.GARTHWAITE	C.STOKES	PARKER	14
3	T.A.PEARCE	ST.BRIDGE	MADAR	61
4	E.F.FINCHER	C.MADAR	STOKES	0
5	A.H.MADAR	B	PARKER	0
6	K.NAZARIN	C.MADAR	PARKER	14
7	D.W.PERSE	C & B	MADAR	17
8	E.L.GOSANO	NOT	OUT	33
9	G.R.CLEGG-HILL	C.STOKES	MADAR	2
10	A.R.MINU	C.BOOTH	MADAR	8
11	R.LEE	C.BARSON	MADAR	10
	EXTRAS			6
				175

Bowler	O	M	R	Wd	NB	W
L.F.STOKES	13	5	30	1	-	2
H.V.PARKER	23	6	68	-	-	3
J.B.H.LECKIE	8	3	19	-	-	0
P.MADAR	9	1	35	-	-	5
H.P.MESTON	4	0	17	-	-	0

SHANGHAI WON BY 217 RUNS

(*Overleaf*) Early 20th century view over Central showing the Chater Road ground.

Kong were also reaching the end of an era with the final appearance of Dick Hancock, who since his Interport debut in 1901 had been such an inspiration to cricket in the territory. Hancock, had the satisfaction of bowing out on a winning note. He was to continue to serve on the selection committee and to be president of the HKCC until his death in 1948.

Hancock and his brother, Harry, had been key figures in the 1904 victory in a triangular tournament against Shanghai and a team from the Straits Settlement. Perhaps Dick Hancock's finest knock came in 1914 when he made a defiant unbeaten second innings of 71. It was not enough to stave off defeat but cemented his place as one of the outstanding pre-war players.

Among other Hong Kong stalwarts who stamped their mark on the series were Harry Owen-Hughes, E.B. 'Lobster' Reed and Acky Bowker — all of whom were prominent figures in league cricket in the territory.

In typically forthright manner, Owen-Hughes burst on to the Interport scene in the 1923 clash which saw Tam Pearce making his match-winning 145. During that game Owen-Hughes, a linchpin of the HKCC for several decades, captured 10 wickets with his cleverly flighted slow left-arm deliveries.

Reed and Bowker were both instrumental in the victories of 1924 and 1925. Reed took four wickets in each innings of the 1924 success, while Bowker — who was to be the mainstay of the Hong Kong attack throughout the '20s and early '30s — also finished the match with eight victims to his name.

Bowker, often referred to as an energetic cricketer known for his agile and enthusiastic fielding, was to produce several notable performances with the ball, including a devastating spell in the 1929 match which brought him seven wickets.

Another Hong Kong player who will forever be remembered is Captain John Dunn, one of the 11 cricketers to perish on the SS Bokhara. Dunn had announced himself as a class batsman with an unbeaten 45 in the high-scoring draw of 1891 — one of only two matches between the teams which

1920. The Hong Kong and Shanghai teams in Hong Kong.

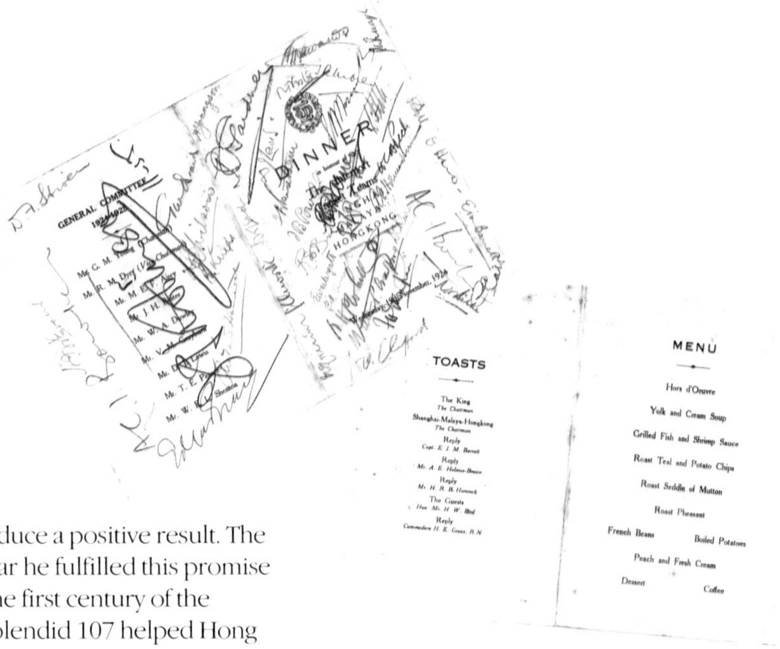
GENERAL COMMITTEE

DINNER

HONGKONG

TOASTS

The King
The Chairman
Shanghai-Malaya-Hongkong
The Chairman
Reply
Capt. E. I. M. Barrett
Reply
Mr. A. E. Holmes-Brown
Reply
Mr. H. R. B. Hancock
The Guests
Hon. Mr. H. W. Bird
Reply
Commodore H. E. Grace, R.N.

MENU

Hors d'Oeuvre
Yolk and Cream Soup
Grilled Fish and Shrimp Sauce
Roast Teal and Potato Chips
Roast Saddle of Mutton
Roast Pheasant
French Beans — Boiled Potatoes
Peach and Fresh Cream
Dessert — Coffee

failed to produce a positive result. The following year he fulfilled this promise by scoring the first century of the series. His splendid 107 helped Hong Kong to a resounding victory by an innings and 132 runs at Chater Road. But the tables were turned later in the year when Shanghai scored an overwhelming home triumph, although the match was to pale into insignificance in the aftermath of the Bokhara tragedy.

Not surprisingly, the Bokhara disaster slowed the progress of the series, and it was not until November 1897 that the matches resumed. Needing 201 to win in the last innings, Hong Kong seemed to be staring defeat in the face when last man A. Arthur joined P.A. Cox in the middle. However, Cox, later to become general manager of the Canadian Pacific Railway, skilfully kept the strike and finished with an undefeated 38 to give his team a tense one-wicket win.

Fittingly, the first match in February 1866 between the Shanghai visitors and the 'civilians of Hong Kong' produced a record which was to stand throughout the 82-year history of the series. Showing no sympathy to a Shanghai team exhausted from their arduous journey, Hong Kong recorded the first, and by far the easiest, of their 21 victories. Aided by the travel-weary Shanghai bowlers, who sent down no fewer than 41 wides, Hong Kong totalled a daunting 430. They then twice dismissed the visitors cheaply to win the match by an innings and 264 runs, a margin of victory which was never surpassed.

Nevertheless, Shanghai were quick to extract revenge when they entertained Hong Kong the following year. Experiencing the same difficulty acclimatising after the trip as their opponents had in 1866, Hong Kong were soundly beaten in two days. There was then a gap of 22 years before the contest was resumed in Shanghai.

Shanghai maintained the 100 per cent record of the host teams on a rain-affected wicket which made batting hazardous and was responsible for preventing either side reaching three figures. Only Frank Maitland, a future president of the HKCC, showed the necessary application in a painstaking innings of 38. Requiring just 55 to win, Shanghai struggled desperately and eventually scraped in by three wickets.

In 1903, Tam Pearce made his first appearance in a game which was highlighted by a match-winning innings of 136 by Hong Kong's Lieutenant Lumsden. Pearce never lost his desire for run-scoring and he quickly made up for lost time with a century on Armistice Day in 1920 when the series started up again following a six-year break.

Kent county player Alec Pearce, Tam's son, made his Interport debut in 1933 with a significant contribution to Hong Kong's success in the triangular tournament. Although primarily a batsman, Pearce Junior made his mark as a third change bowler, capturing six second innings wickets. A courageous innings of 83 from Tom Hayward, who batted throughout with a broken finger, had laid the foundation for victory.

The form book went out of the window in 1934 when a powerful Hong Kong team, tipped to score a comfortable victory, was given a severe thrashing in Shanghai. Perhaps the shaky journey which saw the visitors arrive one day late after being caught in a typhoon was partly to blame.

Leonard Stokes, who joined the HKCC after World War II, punished the Hong Kong bowling in a masterly innings of 161 followed by a half-century in the second innings. The only Hong Kong bowler to emerge with credit was giant former Oxford goalkeeper G.R.M. Ricketts, who used his height to extract lift and bounce, and claimed eight wickets.

Hong Kong's 31-run win in 1935 was memorable for the fact that father

1920. Hong Kong vs Malaya.

1914. The Hong Kong XI in Shanghai.

and son, Tam and Alec Pearce, played together for the only time. The final pre-war match in 1936 saw Hong Kong on the wrong end of a heavy reversal. John Leckie (who followed Alec Pearce as the HKCC president) with 80 and a century from number nine H.V. Parker, enabled Shanghai to top 400. Ernie Fincher made an excellent ton in reply but lacked support and Hong Kong, for whom the Indian Recreation Club's A.R. Minu delivered 94 overs, were well beaten.

The battle resumed in 1947 with many of the old stalwarts from both sides still to the fore — Stokes and versatile all-rounder Leach particularly prominent in defeat for Shanghai. History was made again in 1948 when for the first time Hong Kong travelled by air in what proved to be the final meeting of the teams.

Had it not been for a special concession from the US Navy to make the Shanghai ground available for the Interport, the great Frank Howarth would have been denied the opportunity of joining the long list of distinguished names who took part in the series. It did not take the off-spinner long to assert his authority with a match haul of 10 wickets as Shanghai crumbled to 35 all out in the last innings — the lowest score on record. It was also fitting that Alec Pearce, whose father Tam had made his debut 45 years earlier, Owen-Hughes and Leach, who moved to Hong Kong and for many years did a sterling job as grounds convenor at Chater Road, all played in that match.

Although that was to be the last occasion the teams met on the cricket field, following the closure of the Shanghai club, the HKCC became Shanghai's headquarters with their old members given permanent membership at Chater Road. And the tradition of friendliness between the clubs is maintained to this day with two wreaths — one from the HKCC and one from Shanghai — laid each year on Remembrance Day. ■

Shanghai Cricket Club. 1930
To Eric Mitchell from old Shanghai cricket friends with many pleasant memories of days in the China sun.
Solly Shroff
Tony Chandler

Ray Holgate

BOKHARA

Monday 10th October 1892 will always be remembered as the blackest day in the history of Hong Kong cricket. On that fateful day, the SS Bokhara, a P & O steamship with 148 people on board, sank off Sand Island in the Pascaderes killing all but 23 of the passengers. Eleven of those who perished were members of the Hong Kong cricket team returning from the Interport in Shanghai.

Under the command of Captain Charles Dawson Sams, the sturdy 2,940-ton Bokhara set sail from Shanghai at noon on Saturday 8th October on a 1,600-mile journey south. It never made its intended destination. Despite a customary north-east monsoon as the Bokhara pulled out of Shanghai there was no indication of the tragedy that was to unfold.

However, the weather deteriorated to such an extent on the Sunday that Captain Sams decided he could no longer maintain his course. By nightfall the barometer fell rapidly and the wind rose indicating the approach of a typhoon. Fighting a losing battle with the fierce gale, the ship was being steadily driven towards the north-west coast of Formosa, now Taiwan.

The sails were furled. The engines were set to dead slow and the ship brought to the wind on a port tack. By 6 am on Monday it was decided that the ship be put on the other tack in a desperate bid to rescue the situation. The tiring crew failed in their efforts Laying beam on to the sea with her engines stopped, the Bokhara underwent a frightful battering.

One by one her lifeboats and deck fittings were smashed and either blown or swept away as she drifted across the Taiwan Straits. The captain tried vainly to bring her head around, but she drove on helplessly. By Monday evening everyone was near giving up hope. In a last-ditch attempt to abate the heavy seas, Captain Sams ordered oil to be pumped everboard.

For a brief moment it had the desired effect, but the oil flow soon stopped as a result of blocked pipes. At about 9:30 pm, three monster waves broke in succession over the Bokhara. Water cascaded down. The engine room skylights were shattered, the

The Hong Kong and Shanghai cricket teams in 1892.

fires were doused and the machinery flodded.

It was almost midnight when land was spotted no more than a few hundred yards away. While Captain Sams went below to warn the passengers, the engineers heroically attempted to get the fires started again. It was all to no avail. Within minutes, the Bokhara struck Sand Island. As the ship smashed into the island for a second time her side was ripped wide open. In less than two minutes there was no trace of her.

Only two of the 25 survivors were passengers — both members of the Hong Kong cricket team. They were Docter Lowson of the Government Civil Hospital and Lieutenant Markham of the Shropshire Light Infantry. Those who survived were taken to the nearby island of Ponghou where they were looked after by the villagers before being picked up a few days later.

Unaware of the disaster, families and friends of the passengers began to worry when the Bokhara failed to arrive in Hong Kong. Numerous vessels set out in search, but it was a full week before confirmation of the catastrophe reached Hong Kong. On Monday 17th October, a telegram arrived from Swatow. It stated: "Saved — Lowson." Hopes that all were safe increased when Lowson sent a second telegram later in the day. "On board Porpoise, arrive tomorrow." The hope was short-lived. Later that afternoon Captain Burr of HMS Porpoise sent a telegram stating that the Bokhara had been totally wrecked off Sand Island in heavy seas and about 125 people had lost their lives.

He said only 25 had been saved, including the Chief Officer, Third and Fourth Officers, two European quartermasters, two European passengers (Dr. Lowson and Lt. Markham) and 18 Asiatics, among them some members of the crew. The Porpoise arrived in Hong Kong the following day with the survivors.

The reaction of Hong Kong's expatriate community was of profound shock and horror. A relief committee was set up under the Governor, subscriptions raised and memorial services held. Public anger mounted that more had not been done to save the vessel and that the memorial service was advertised in a newspaper.

The first outcry arose following a remark from Dr. Lowson to reporters upon his return. It was subsequently denied by Lowson and other survivors who were adamant that every possible measure had been taken to save the Bokhara. The advertisment was greeted with general disapproval and was described in a China Mail editorial as "like selling Pears soap".

The Bokhara monument was erected by the Navy on Sand Island in 1893, while a stained glass memorial window, from funds raised by the Shanghai Cricket Club, was placed in the south aisle of St John's Cathedral in Hong Kong. The window, removed during the Japanese occupation, consists of two lights.

The western one has a full length picture of St. Paul with a scene underneath of his shipweck. The eastern shows a representation of St. Peter walking on the water. On the pier between the two lights is fixed a brass plate with the following inscription:

In token of their Deep Regret for the Loss of Major Turner, APD; Capt J. Dunn, ASC; Capt Dawson, Hong Kong Regiment; Lieutenant Burnett, 53rd Regiment; Lieutenant G.G. Boyle, RA; Sergeant Donegan, 53rd Regiment; Sergeant Mumford, 53rd Regiment; Quartermaster-Sergeant Jeffkins, RE; G.S. Purvis, Esq; G.E. Taverner, Esq; C. Wallace, Esq.

Members of the Hong Kong Cricket Team who Perished in the Wreck of the P and O Steamer Bokhara, on 10th October, 1892, while on their Return Voyage to Hong Kong after the Interport Cricket Match.

No other Cathedral in the world contains a memorial to members of a cricket team, and we trust that no occasion will arise for one to be erected.

Lieutenant Markham stayed on in the Army and was promoted to Captain before he died in London in May 1909. Doctor Lowson was so severely affected by the shock and exposure that he had to retire from the Civil Service. He eventually settled in Scotland. ■

(Overleaf) Looking northward across the Parade Ground toward the first pavilion in the late 19th century.

The Bokhara Shield.

TOURISTS

Few non first-class cricket playing nations can have enjoyed the privilege of playing host to so many of the game's great names and characters as Hong Kong. Since Jack Chegwyn led an Australian Test team to the territory to celebrate the 100th anniversary of the HKCC in 1952, a never-ending stream of the sport's super stars has ventured East.

In addition to the forging of many longstanding friendships, the tourists have provided Hong Kong's leading players with an opportunity to perform against them while giving hours of pleasure to the territory's cricket fans. The obvious joy players such as Bobby Simpson, Harold Larwood, Geoff Boycott, Tom Graveney, Gary Sobers and Sonny Ramadhin — to name but a few — have derived from parading their talents at Chater Road and more recently Wong Nai Chung Gap Road has done more than anything to put Hong Kong on the world cricketing map.

Such is the popularity of the place and the hospitality which is afforded visiting teams and players that Hong Kong has become one of the most sought-after stopover points for Test, county and club cricketers. Indeed, Hong Kong's status as a quality cricketing venue was confirmed in December 1986, when the world all-rounders Silk Cut Challenge — featuring Imran Khan, Richard Hadlee, Clive Rice, Graham Gooch and Madan Lal — was staged at the HKCC. The spectacular views across the harbour were featured almost as prominently as the cricket itself in a two-hour television documentary screened in the United Kingdom early in January 1987.

For those professional cricketers fortunate enough to have played there, the unique setting and inimitable character of the Chater Road ground was as exciting an experience as performing in front of capacity crowds at any of the world's great Test venues. During his year in office as president of the Marylebone Cricket Club and chairman of the International Cricket Conference, Colin Cowdrey, England's most-capped Test player, visited the territory and summed up the feelings of many when he recalled his impressions of stepping out to the wicket at Chater Road.

(Top) 1975. Match in progress between the Australian Super Stars and the HKCA President's XI at Chater Road.
(Bottom left) 1975. Bobby Simpson and Richard Mills-Owen in the Australian Super Stars match.
(Bottom right) 1975. Peter Davies and Noel Hooper in the Australian Super Stars match.

HONG KONG v. M. C. C.

THURSDAY 13-3-75

STANDING

D. KHAN (UMPIRE), A. KNOTT, R. SABNANI (SCORER) R. LALCHANDANI, R. STARLING, R. TAYLOR, M. BULFIELD, J. BYGATE, D. UNDERWOOD, I. STEVENS, B. WOOD, D. AMISS, B. LUCKHURST, M. HENDRICKS, O. ROBINSON, C. OLD, G. LALCHANDANI, B. KWONG, G. BUTLER, F. TITMUS, H. MELLOWES (UMPIRE), T. WILLSON.

SITTING

A. SMITH, A. GREIG, C. MYATT, W. CONWAY, M. DENNESS, J. SHROFF, A. BEDSER.

H.K.C.C. TOUR TO BRITAIN – JULY, 1978

(SIDMOUTH, DEVON)

STANDING

W. CONWAY (Manager) A. BARNETT D. FOSTER D. FORD J. HUGHES M. HISLOP R. MULREADY B. HEMSHALL "BADGER" SMITH D. MINNS R. TOES T. HENDERSON

SEATED

M. LEWIS M. DARKE G. FOSTER P. DAVIES (Capt.) M. BULFIELD K. SILLETT I. STEVENS

1975. The Australian Super Stars vs the HKCC at Chater Road

"It was a fantastic experience and I don't think there could ever have been another ground anywhere else in the world quite like it," said Cowdrey, who scored a typically polished 46 for the MCC in 1966. Mention Hong Kong to any of the Test greats who graced Chater Road and the indelible memories stamped on their minds come flooding back. Such was the aura of the place and the friendliness of the HKCC members that numerous players were 'adopted' by the Club and frequently pay fleeting visits to renew acquaintances.

But it was after the success of Chegwyn's 1952 tour, that word quickly spread of the appeal of playing in Hong Kong. Unquestionably the most historic tour was made by the Australian Super Stars in April 1975, when Ian Johnson brought a powerful squad to play four matches and bring down the curtain on the HKCC's 124 years at Chater Road.

Sir Denys Roberts, president of the Club, writing in the commemorative programme said: "The Super Stars delighted us with the skills which have given pleasure to millions of people in the past. They endowed our closing matches, which might have been a sad occasion, with grace, cheerfulness and distinction. Above all, they were men of charm and humour, who did everything they could to make a success of their tour. This they assuredly achieved, and in their short stay they made very many friends. It was a happy ending to a great innings."

The grand finale had been planned by Keith Sillett of Cathay Pacific Airways. And what a week it was as the superb selection of great Australian players from the previous 50 years won the hearts of all who met them and watched them perform. The galaxy of stars included Ian Johnson, Ian Craig, Bobby Simpson, Neil Harvey, Alan Davidson, Ray Lindwall, Ron Archer, Jim Burke, Bill Brown, Les Favell, Peter Philpott, Ian Meckiff and Rodney Marsh.

Also present, although not in a playing capacity, were 83-year-old Clarrie Grimmett, Bert Oldfield and Harold Larwood, as well as Jack Chegwyn whose 1952 tour had cemented cricketing relations between the countries. Oldfield, one of the

most accomplished wicket-keepers of all time, made an emotional speech before the Australians returned home. "Let me say on behalf of all cricketers throughout the world and the Super Stars in particular that I do not ever remember enjoying a tour of such happiness. May you take the 125 years of cricket history with you from Chater Road to Wong Nai Chung Gap, and may your club go from strength to strength, always maintaining the real spirit of cricket."

With the Gods smiling and the rain holding off, the players responded by producing some marvellous cricket and memories which will live long in the minds of those who witnessed or took part in the week-long carnival. The excitement and drama began on the very first ball of the opening match when Bobby Simpson was dropped at slip off the bowling of Kit Cummings. Neil Harvey and Jim Burke both scored breathtaking half-centuries enabling the Australians to declare at a mammoth 291 for six. One local critic described Harvey's 65 as "sheer magic and all who witnessed it rejoiced in the poetry of its compilation."

Undaunted, the President's XI hit back strongly. John Baskervyle-Glegg and Jalu Shroff showed scant respect for the bowling and the home team began Peter Philpott's last over requiring three to win with three wickets standing. They could only manage two with the tie-equalling run fittingly coming from the bat of Sir Denys Roberts.

Simpson, Johnson and Favell were the architects of the Super Stars' 11-run defeat of the HKCC Volunteers on the second day and Simpson again rose to the occasion the following day in a match between Bill Brown's XI and Ian Johnson's XI which both included HKCC members. Simpson scored 103 in 63 minutes including five sixes and 14 fours and then took three wickets to

(*Left*) 1975. Sir Denys Roberts flips the coin, watched by Australian Super Stars captain, Ian Johnson.
(*Bottom*) 1975. Members of the HKCC and Australian Super Stars XIs.

take Brown's team to a 57-run triumph. In keeping with the rest of the week, the final match — HKCC versus Super Stars — turned into a thriller and a fitting climax to the tour.

Skipper Peter Davies and Noel Hooper posted a century stand to get the HKCC off to a flying start and set the scene for the outstanding innings of Peter Green's life. Following an uncertain beginning, the Scorpions man cut loose to hammer 95 in better than even time and leave the Super Stars needing 237 for victory at almost a run a minute. With Simpson again in marvellous form making 85 in 38 minutes, the game seemed over. But back came HKCC with John Ashworth and Roger Mulready slicing through the middle order. At 157 for five the match hung in the balance, but Marsh and Davidson then called on their experience as the Australians reached their target with four wickets in hand.

Also during 1975, the MCC stopped off in Hong Kong on their way back from Australia and played at Chater Road where they fielded a full Test side — Dennis Amiss, Barry Wood, Tony Greig, Alan Knott, Chris Old, Bob Taylor, Mike Denness, Brian Luckhurst, Fred Titmus, Derek Underwood and Mike Hendrick. And they showed little sympathy for the Hong Kong team as they amassed 234 for three with Amiss making 101 and Wood 68. The home side was then dismissed for 132 with Titmus and Underwood each taking four wickets.

After the pioneering tour of Chegwyn's Australians it was not until 1962 that another Test strength team came to Hong Kong to play against a full Colony side. The Commonwealth XI, with Tom Graveney, Bobby Simpson and Sonny Ramadhin all delighting the crowd with their skills, recorded a 35-run victory despite a brave half-century from former Colony skipper David Coffey.

Two years later, West Indian Gary Sobers made his debut in the territory

(Top) Amongst the most distinguished cricket visitors has been Sir Garfield Sobers (third from left) — arguably the greatest all-rounder.
(Right) 1987. MCC Bi-centenary dinner at Wong Nai Chung Gap. From left: Jamie Barber, Colin Cowdrey, Sir Denys Roberts, John Bygate, Norman Ludlow.

with another Commonwealth team and in typical fashion won the two-innings game almost single-handedly with match figures of nine for 70 and a brilliant century. Although Sobers played in Hong Kong on several occasions he did not always meet with success. Ian Lacy-Smith, a giant left-arm fast bowler who has been a member of the HKCC since the early 1960s, will forever cherish the memory when he dismissed the great man during the 1964 tour of E. W. Swanton's International XI.

Playing for the Commander of British Forces XI, Lacy-Smith had the distinction of removing Colin Ingleby-MacKenzie, the Nawab of Pataudi and Sobers before 30 runs were on the board. From 140 for eight, Swanton's XI recovered thanks to some hard hitting by Richie Benaud and Ken Taylor and were eventually bowled out for 243. With Sobers, Benaud and Sonny Ramadhin bowling flat out, the visitors prevailed. On the same tour, Soberts vented his anger after Dr. Alex Delikhan had bowled him first ball by taking five Malayan wickets in five balls spread over two overs.

Twenty-three years earlier, Chegwyn's team had been surprised to discover so many talented players in Hong Kong. Major Tom Haycraft took a century off them at Chater Road although his outstanding effort was overshadowed by the antics of Keith Miller. Never one to shirk a challenge, Miller could not resist the temptation of trying to break one of the windows of the imposing Bank of China building with a six. As soon as he reached the crease, Miller launched into the bowlers and middled one which soared towards the bank. To his dismay, the ball crashed against the wall, narrowly missing the window. He was dismissed shortly afterwards and walked back to the pavilion shaking his head in disappointment.

Even in 1905, cricket was sufficiently popular to warrant media coverage of the visit of a legendary English star of that era — Lord Hawke, whose cousin R.E.O. Bird was a left-arm bowler who represented Hong Kong in several Interports before the War. The South China Morning Post reported on 11th March 1905: "The visit

(Top) Members of New Zealand's national side go through exercises at Wong Nai Chung Gap. *(Bottom)* 1985. Ten years at Wong Nai Chung Gap. From left: Les Favell, Neil Harvey, Sir Denys Roberts, Ian Craig, Ray Lindwall, Keith Sillett.

of Lord Hawke created quite a stir among the local wielders of willow. He arrived on the P & O steamer Nubia and was accompanied by Mr M.C. Bonsor. The Nubia did not arrive till 5 o'clock. Mr E.W. Mitchell, president of the HKCC, and Mr A.R. Lowe, secretary and treasurer, set out to meet and welcome the distinguished pair."

Two days later the Yorkshire County Cricket Club captain and England player was in action at Chater Road. "On the Cricket Ground on Saturday teams representing the HKCC and the Ladies Recreation Club met, the match being of special interest in that Lord Hawke took a place on the Club side. Play opened before tiffin and the Hong Kong team went into bat, Lord Hawke and T.E. (Tam) Pearce being the first batsmen. It was a little disappointing to see the central figure of the match dismissed very early for the small score of two runs by R. Hancock. Lord Hawke had evidently not got his eye in, and it is to be hoped another match will be arranged before his departure so that local cricket enthusiasts may see him in better form," the paper reported.

December 1986. The Silk Cut Challenge at Wong Nai Chung Gap. Clockwise from top left: Clive Rice, Imran Khan, Madan Lal, Graham Gooch, Richard Hadlee.

In April, 1965, the visitors were English County Championship winners Worcestershire who were celebrating their success with a world tour. Their star-studded team was practically of Test class. Skippered by Don Kenyon they also included Martin Horton, Ron Headley (son of West Indian great, George), Dick Richardson, Tom Graveney, Basil d'Oliveira, Roy Booth, Doug Slade, Norman Gifford and pacemen Les Flavell and Len Coldwell.

A green Chater Road track offered plenty of encouragement for the fast bowlers in a match against a Hong Kong Cricket Association President's XI. Kenyon was given an early shock when his cap was knocked off by a bouncer and as he trudged back to the pavilion soon after, having been caught at gully, he was heard to murmur: "Wait till Flavell and Coldwell get on this pitch." Graveney, in typically elegant fashion, held the Worcestershire innings together with a chanceless century and finished the innings with three successive straight sixes into Chater Road. Then, as Kenyon had predicted, the fireworks began. Coldwell dug one in short which reared up and struck Hong Kong batsman Buji Dhabher just below the eye. The Hong Kong team finished bruised and beaten.

The MCC paid their first visit to the territory in 1966 on the way back from their tour of Australia. Yorkshire opener Geoff Boycott, who made several subsequent trips to Hong Kong, marked the occasion with a century to put his team in the driving seat. Although David Coffey offered stout resistance in an excellent innings of 88, the pace of Jeff Jones combined with the spin of David Allen proved too much for the home side which was beaten.

Visiting MCC officials at the HKCC. From left: T.A. Pearce (HKCC president), Lord Nugent (MCC president), G.O. Allen (former captain of England).

Among the most prominent cricketing memories of Sir Denys Roberts is a match at Chater Road in late 1967 when he skippered the President's XI against the Cricket Club of India. Batting first, the tourists, captained by 'Polly' Umrigar, began well with K.S. Indrajitsinhji, a wicket-keeper-batsman who won four Test caps, striking the ball sweetly. The Indian launched himself into another full-blooded off-drive which looked like bringing him a further boundary. But Sir Denys, who had strategically placed himself at deep mid-off as he contemplated how to stop the flow of runs, was unable to get out of the way and to the disbelief of the crowd pulled off a memorable catch.

In the main match of that tour the CCI were held to a draw, but 1968 saw Hong Kong slump to their heaviest ever defeat in a two innings game against a powerful International XI. Six

1975. The Australian Super Stars vs the HKCC at Chater Road

players — Billy Ibadulla, Mike Denness, Dennis Amiss, Harry Latchman, Geoff Arnold and Micky Stewart — all made more than 40 to take their team to 353 all out. Latchman, Harold Rhodes and Derek Underwood then destroyed Hong Kong for 66 and 73.

Hong Kong's frailty against top-class spinners was repeatedly exposed throughout the 1970s. Never, though, was it more apparent than when they entertained the D.H. Robins XI in 1977. Having restricted them to 167, Hong Kong then collapsed against the three-pronged spin attack of Pakistan's Intikhab Alam and England duo John Emburey and Peter Willey. It was a similar story two years later when Surrey came to visit and between them, leg-spinner Intikhab and off-break bowler Pat Pocock claimed eight wickets for just 57 runs.

The 1979 tour of the Australians provided another landmark and a chance for many of their players to see the HKCC's new home at Wong Nai Chung Gap. The line-up was virtually a 'Who's Who' of Australian cricket through the years. Between them the tourists had clocked up in excess of 600 Test caps, scoring thousands of runs and taking hundreds of wickets. They boasted no fewer than eight former captains — Lindsay Hassett, Ian Johnson, Arthur Morris, Neil Harvey, Brian Booth, Ian Craig, Bill Brown and Ray Lindwall — while seven of the squad had played in Sir Donald Bradman's all-conquering 1948 team.

Further visits by the MCC and more recently the New Zealand Test team have added to Hong Kong's reputation as a flourishing cricket outpost. It is impossible to measure the goodwill that has been built up between touring sides and their hosts or the joy that so many have derived from the visits. There are precious few places in the world where club players have regular opportunities to pit their skills against the very best. Hong Kong is an exception to the rule and those who have bowled to Boycott or faced Sobers or even simply stood on the same field will forever cherish the memories. Long may it continue. ■

(Overleaf) Chater Road ground, looking south with the first pavilion in the right foreground.

OTHER SPORTS

Resourcefulness and resilience are qualities the Hong Kong Cricket Club's Lawn Bowls section have always possessed in abundance. Without them it is unlikely they would ever have been formed and almost certain they would not have survived. And it is testament to the dedication of their officials and players that they are now accepted as such an integral part of the Club, whose initial reservations about allowing the formation of the bowls section have forever been allayed.

Indeed, the bowlers, who celebrated their 50th anniversary in 1986, have established themselves to such an extent that they currently enjoy a status as arguably the most thriving sporting section at the Club. Yet any such suggestions in the mid-1930s would have been greeted with uproarious laughter from the cricketers of that era. When it was suggested that at the end of the 1935 season a lawn should be made available at the cricket ground for use between the cricket seasons, it was met with vehement protest and howls of disapproval from a large section of the membership.

"The Committee of the HKCC were by no means favourable to the idea and some of the stalwart cricketers were decidedly antagonistic," reported the Hon. P.S. Cassidy in an article in the Club's centenary handbook. Perhaps it was a mixture of jealous resentment that they might have to share their facilities, and the fear of outsiders invading their hallowed Club and encroaching on their territory that brought about such deep felt opposition from the cricketers to the proposal.

Nevertheless, the arguments for such a move were sound and well-founded. The vast majority of those who backed the proposal were Club members who had represented the Royal Hong Kong Yacht Club at bowls. When the Yacht Club green, which was attached to the clubhouse in North Point, had to be given up in 1935 the bowlers were forced to look for a new venue. With the connections at the HKCC, Chater Road became the number-one target for the bowlers to be re-housed.

Following numerous heated discussions on the subject, the Committee grudgingly agreed to allow

(Top) 1966. HKCC lawn bowls team which gained promotion to the HKLBA First Division for the first time in the Club's history.
(Right) Car park with rooftop tennis court.

the bowlers a trial period. "After a good deal of pressure had been applied the Committee gave a reluctant consent, but on certain conditions," recalled Cassidy. "One was that no ditches could be cut across the sacred turf and that tapes should be used as a substitute. This meant that the green could not be used for league matches so further pressure was necessary."

Cassidy continued: "Ultimately the Committee gave way, but insisted that the ditches could not be cut before April 15 and would have to be filled in by September 15." Hardly surprisingly, relations between the bowlers and cricketers, who today live happily hand in hand, were strained and according to Cassidy "the original lawn bowlers were regarded as intruders and it took some little time for them to establish themselves as respectable members of the Club."

Although the bowls section was officially conceived in 1936 when two teams were entered in the league — one in the Second Division and one in the Third — the results were far from spectacular. Despite the lack of success, the green (part of the cricket outfield situated in a far corner of the ground bounded by Chater Road and Murray Road, was among the most popular in Hong Kong.

In a short time it earned a reputation as a true, reliable green with excellent drainage. The fact that it was fenced by open iron railings made play easily visible to inquisitive passers-by. Such was the concentration of the bowlers, however, that they generally remained oblivious to those who peered through the gaps. Some still vividly recall the occasion during the 1967 riots when the ground was surrounded by angry mobs which were gathering in Central. The hardy bowlers, not wanting to be disturbed from their practice, hardly raised an eyebrow. "It would have taken more than that to put us off our game," said Alan Bailey, a prominent member of the Club since 1958.

An aged banyan tree half-way between the clubhouse and the green, as well as adding to the character of the ground, had other uses for the bowlers. Alan Johnson, writing in the September 1985 special edition of the Club magazine, the Pinkun, to celebrate 10 years at Wong Nai Chung

Gap, described the tree as a "wondrous arboreal masterpiece". He continued: "In its day, this fine tree afforded shelter for bowlers during rain showers and a canopy for the portable bar from which cold drinks were served."

As well as staging league and friendly matches and the annual Club Championship knockout singles and pairs, Chater Road was used for the National Championships in which male and female gold medallists from the world and Commonwealth championships took part. Setbacks such as relegation and typhoon-inflicted damage to the posts supporting the bowling green floodlights were overcome in the typically matter-of-fact and forthright fashion which has always been a hallmark of the section.

Those characteristics were never more evident than during the move to Wong Nai Chung Gap. It was at that time that the resolve, spirit and selfless hard work — which their counterparts of 40 years previous had shown to get the bowling section off the ground — again came to the fore. With the turf from Chater Road having been cut up

(Top) Men's 'B' tennis team, 1986.
(Bottom) Men's 'D' tennis team, 1986.

1984. Members of the HKCC syndicate with 'Major Irish', winner of the Birmingham Handicap.

(Top) Happy Valley. View from the HKCC race box.
(Right) 1984. Members of the HKCC syndicate with 'Major Irish', winner of the Lion Rock Handicap.

and transferred to the new site in 1974, the resilient bowlers were very much left to fend for themselves.

Unforeseen problems, arose as were reported in the Pinkun. "The first attempt at laying the bowling green in 1974 seemed to succeed — until quite suddenly, following heavy rain and tropical sunshine, a banana tree shot up in the middle of the green. It was promptly lopped at its base. However, within a fortnight the triffid-like creature reappeared! Mr Chu and Drains attacked the beast with a vengeance, pick-axes and shovels, to a depth of one metre. Hopefully the dreaded creature will not reappear."

With the move having gone through in July 1975 the bowlers were in a quandary with the green clearly unfit for play. However, the graciousness of Kowloon Bowling Green Club and Kowloon Dock Club in offering their greens as an alternative 'home' venue provided the HKCC with a lifeline which was gratefully accepted. Remarkably in the circumstances, the Club fielded three full men's teams and a ladies' team in the league.

Although the men's third team had to withdraw before the end of the season and the Club knockout was postponed, it was a memorable year for John McNie and David McKenzie who won the Colony Inter-Hong pairs title — following in the footsteps of Barry Manchester and Bob Bone, who in 1970-71 became the first HKCC players to win a Colony crown. By the start of the 1976 season, the Gap green was finally ready for use.

It was very much a season of contrast. Although there were reasons for celebration — the resumption of Club tournaments, a narrow win for Bob Suttie against Tim Henderson in the singles final, the first of three successive victories for Immer Kermani in the Julie Johnson-presented rosebowl trophy for the ladies' singles and the performance of Robert Barnett in reaching the final of the Hong Kong Junior singles championship — there was also disappointment.

The first team, which had become accustomed to alternately gaining promotion from the Second Division and then immediately being relegated from the First, suffered the ignominy

General view of Wong Nai Chung Gap ground with lawn bowls, cricket nets and tennis facilities.

of going down to the Third Division for the first time. Consolidating the playing strength by reducing league participation to one team, HKCC, under the convenorship of Jim Viney, finished runners-up in 1978 to regain their Second Division status.

Inspired by John Stewart, who won the Club singles, pairs and Younghusband competition as well as representing the Club as a trialist for selection in the World Bowls tournament, the Second Division team finished fourth while the second team re-entered the Third Division. Since then fortunes have been mixed. Departures and unavailability (problems which have dogged the bowling section since its inception) conspired to provide more frustration and it was not until 1984 that promotion to the Second Division was gained again.

Through all the ups and downs, the social side has continued to flourish thanks to the unstinting support of the bowling members. One of the highlights is the annual Younghusband knockout which, like the Barnes Decanter for ladies' pairs, the Richardson Trophy for mixed triples, the Johnstone Cup for mixed rinks and the Simpson Shield for mixed pairs, enjoys a large entry and enthusiastic support.

John Johnstone, the Club's Lawn Bowls representative until 1986, succinctly appraised the role and success of the bowls section in a 50th anniversary message. "By success I do not mean (nor could I mean) our achievements on the field of play where we have had our ups and downs from season to season and from week to week. Indeed, given the ever-increasing demands on individuals' time and, in some cases, their predilections for competing forms of leisure activity, our playing achievements have been consistent only in their inconsistency. Rather, the success of lawn bowls at the Club should be seen in terms of the position it occupies as a focal point for social activity and enjoyment in the lives of those who play."

Of all the sporting facilities within the Club, the greatest progress — in terms of facilities and the amount of members who make use of them — has come in the squash section. From the handful of enthusiasts who represented the Club at Victoria

(Top) 1987-88 'Champion Masters' squash team (one mistress!).
(Bottom) The 'All Stars' soccer team: "wildly exaggerated reports in the Pinkun".

Barracks and Victoria Park during the 1960s has grown a massive band of players who take full advantage of Wong Nai Chung Gap's squash complex which includes four courts.

The rise to prominence of the squash section has coincided with the move from Chater Road and the dramatic increase in the popularity of the sport in Hong Kong over the past decade. If judged by the quantity of those who use them, there can be no doubt that the decision to build four courts — instead of two as had originally been planned — at the Gap has been fully vindicated.

The present-day comforts such as air-conditioning and showers (conspicious by their absence in the Victoria Barracks days) have been significant factors in attracting members to take an active interest in the sport. Although the strength in depth of the squash section has never been greater, the Chater Road days did bring numerous pieces of silverware to the Club.

With Martin Clinch, a Colony champion, heading the list of players, the Club twice won the Second Division championship although it was never able to make an impression in the top flight. However, since the move, the Club has lifted the First Division title on two occasions. John Cooper, another former Hong Kong champion, dominated the scene for a couple of years in the mid-'70s while other Club champions include Neil Speakman, Joe Chow, Neil Goodman-Smith, Chris Charles and Dave Beaumont.

During its short history, the women's section has also stamped its mark on the sport in Hong Kong. The team of Julie Michelmore, Liz Petts, Karil Greenhalgh, Beatriz Tancock and Barbara Marrett were champions of the First Division in 1984-85.

Since 1977, the Club has run its own internal summer league and in 1982 the women's winter league was formed. Currently, the Club fields no fewer than 10 men's and four women's teams in the Hong Kong winter leagues, while between 10 and 12 teams made up of Club members take part in the internal summer leagues.

(Left) 'Après cricket' in the Chater Tavern.
(Bottom) John Lunn, HKCC snooker singles champion.

Members of the staff who received 10-year service medallions from Sir Denys Roberts at the Ten Years at the Gap celebrations — 28th September 1985.

Fiftieth anniversary of HKCC lawn bowls games — August 1986.

In contrast to the way in which lawn bowls and squash have proved key growth areas within the Club, tennis has not attracted such widespread involvement — probably due more to a lack of facilities than anything else. Nevertheless, encouraged by the recent addition of an all-weather court on the roof of the new car park, the sport is enjoying a resurgence, particularly as a social activity among wives of members.

The centenary booklet made reference to the fact that the territory's Lawn Tennis Championships had always been held at Chater Road and been organised by the HKCC. When the Hong Kong Lawn Tennis Association was formed in the early 1930s it assumed responsibility for the running of the event, although Chater Road remained very much the home of Hong Kong tennis.

In addition to the Open championship, the HKCC organised its own Club championship and handicap events as well as being regularly represented in the local tennis league. Although tennis has never been one of the Club's major sporting strengths, the men's team of 1929 — including stalwart cricketer and clubman Harry Owen-Hughes, L. Goldman and G.W. Sewell — won the league championship.

The Chater Road grass courts, which were used for Hong Kong's home matches in the Davis Cup as well as being graced by numerous world-ranked playing during stopovers, were acknowledged as the finest in the territory. Indeed, the lush surface with its reliable bounce prompted many famed visitors to favourably compare the courts with those at the All-England Club at Wimbledon.

In many ways the move to Wong Nai Chung Gap provided a welcome shot in the arm for tennis within the Club. While at Chater Road it had proved difficult to complete all the events on grass, the option to switch to the floodlit all-weather court at the Gap encouraged more members to take advantage of the improved facilities.

Those facilities also enabled the Club to spread its sporting wings and cater for an even wider-ranging selection of activities. That, in turn, gave the women the opportunity, which they were quick to grab, of

"HOWZAT!" — the HKCC's own very popular annual revue.

(Top) Netball team, 1985.
(Left) HKCC Ladies I squash team.

Tuesday afternoon Junior Sports.

September Swimming Gala.

Saturday morning Junior Cricket.

breaking down the barriers which had been put up at Chater Road where they were very much neglected. Now, as is evidenced by their contribution to lawn bowls, squash, tennis and cricket in the capacity as scorers, they have clearly broken the male stronghold and stamped their mark.

They now run their own netball team, while regular aerobics classes are staged at the Club. And it is not only 'on the field' where they excel. Although to this day women cannot be elected as members, they have established themselves in many areas.

As well as a Mothers and Toddlers group, there is a Ladies' Sub-committee that has become increasingly involved in organising social events such as poolside barbeques, swimming galas and Christmas parties, and serves as a conduit for passing the views of families to management. The Video Club was originally run voluntarily and exclusively by women for the benefit of all, while Julie Johnson is the editor of the Pinkun.

The children are not forgotten either. For the majority of them, and the women, the swimming pool provides the main centre of attraction although there are ample opportunities for them to use other sporting facilities. Junior cricket practices, and matches against other clubs, are frequently arranged as well as group squash and tennis sessions.

The men have also branched out. Although there is no longer a chess section (which ran in the late 1960s and early '70s), compensation has been found in the hallowed Snooker Room on the first floor which has recently undergone plush renovation.

The women, in fact, even managed to penetrate this historically male stronghold for a few years and the ban which was eventually put on them received widespread criticism in the local press. The other strictly male pastime is soccer. The Club's All Stars team have over the years gained notoriety, not just for their playing achievements but also for the seemingly never-ending stream of super-stars who turn out for them and the wildly exaggerated reports of their exploits which appear in the Club's magazine. ■

THE WAY AHEAD

With less than eight years remaining until the People's Republic of China regain sovereignty of Hong Kong, some cynics are already predicting the demise of sporting clubs in the territory. Indeed, with regard to the Hong Kong Cricket Club analogies are being made to the enforced move from Chater Road to Wong Nai Chung Gap Road.

However, the doom and gloom of many is certainly not shared by officials and senior members of the Club. Quite the opposite, in fact. While acknowledging that minor changes may be inevitable in the long-term, the attitude of the Club — in keeping with tradition — is refreshingly positive.

Instead of dwelling on the 1997 changeover with scepticism and doubt, there is an air of excitement and expectancy about the dawning of another new era. Planning for the future is under way with the Committee united in its determination to continue providing the best possible service to Club members.

All the indications from the Government point to an extension of the lease being granted when the current one expires in 1992 and the confidence of the Club is borne out by the Committee's policy in spending a considerable amount of money in renovating existing facilities and even contemplating further expansion as the first stage in the planned improvement of the Club. While the Committee is single-minded in its desire to keep the emphasis on cricket, the open policy to membership will be maintained. If evidence were required of the Chinese Government's attitude towards cricket, it was provided in abundance by their invitation to a team of former Australian Test stars to partake in a 'Friendship Tour' during August 1988.

It was an unprecedented step which proved to be a resounding success with more than 700 locals turning up in the southern city of Shenzhen for a practice session. Indeed, former Australian captain and current national team coach Bobby Simpson — a man with close ties with the Hong Kong Cricket Club — was so impressed with what he saw that he said one day China could enter the Test arena.

And who's to say it won't be the 'Lord's of the Far East' which will be afforded the privilege of hosting that auspicious occasion. ■

1988. Saturday League match in progress at Wong Nai Chung Gap.

CRICKET CHAMPIONSHIP ROLL.

1908-9	First Division Winner	Hong Kong Cricket Club 'B'
1909-10	First Division Winner	Hong Kong Cricket Club 'A'
1912-13	First Division Winner	Hong Kong Cricket Club 'B'
1913-14	First Division Winner	Hong Kong Cricket Club
1917-18	First Division Winner	Hong Kong Cricket Club
1923-24	First Division Winner	Hong Kong Cricket Club
1928-29	First Division Winner	Hong Kong Cricket Club
1928-29	Second Division Winner	Hong Kong Cricket Club
1929-30	Second Division Winner	Hong Kong Cricket Club
1933-34	First Division Winner	Hong Kong Cricket Club
1934-35	First Division Winner	Hong Kong Cricket Club
1936-37	First Division Winner (Joint)	Hong Kong Cricket Club
1949-50	First Division Winner	HKCC Scorpions
1952-53	First Division Winner	HKCC Scorpions
1959-60	First Division Winner	HKCC Optimists
1963-64	First Division Winner	HKCC Optimists
1964-65	Second Division Winner	HKCC Nomads
1966-67	First Division Winner	HKCC Scorpions
1967-68	First Division Winner	HKCC Scorpions
1967-68	Second Division Winner (Joint)	HKCC Nomads
1968-69	Second Division Winner	HKCC Nomads
1970-71	Rothmans Cup Runners Up	HKCC Scorpions
1971-72	First Division Winner	HKCC Optimists
1971-72	Rothmans Cup Runners Up	HKCC Optimists
1973-74	Sunday League Runners Up	HKCC Optimists
1973-74	Saturday League Winner	HKCC Nomads
1973-74	Saturday League Runners Up	HKCC Witherers
1973-74	Rothmans Cup Winner	HKCC Wanderers
1974-75	Sunday League Runners Up	HKCC Wanderers
1975-76	Saturday League Plate Winner	HKCC Witherers
1976-77	Rothmans Cup Winner	HKCC Optimists
1977-78	Sunday League Winner	HKCC Wanderers
1977-78	Saturday League Winner	HKCC Nomads
1978-79	Sunday League Winner	HKCC Optimists
1978-79	Sunday League Runners Up	HKCC Wanderers
1978-79	Saturday League Cup	HKCC Nomads
1979-80	Sunday League Winner	HKCC Optimists
1979-80	Saturday League Runners Up	HKCC Nomads
1979-80	Gillette Cup Winner	HKCC Nomads
1980-81	Gillette Cup Winner	HKCC Nomads
1980-81	Rothmans Cup Runners Up	HKCC Taverners
1981-82	Sunday League Winner	HKCC Scorpions
1981-82	Sunday League Runners Up	HKCC Optimists
1981-82	Gillette Plate Runners Up	HKCC Nomads
1982-83	Saturday League Winner	HKCC Nomads
1982-83	Saturday League Runners Up	HKCC Witherers
1982-83	Rothmans Cup Winners	HKCC Wanderers
1982-83	Rothmans Cup Runners Up	HKCC Scorpions
1983-84	Sunday League Winner	HKCC Scorpions
1983-84	Sunday League Runners Up	HKCC Optimists
1983-84	Saturday League Winner	HKCC Nomads
1983-84	Gillette Cup Winner	HKCC Nomads
1983-84	Gillette Plate Winner	HKCC Gap Ramblers
1984-85	Saturday League Winner	HKCC Nomads
1984-85	Saturday League Runners Up	HKCC Witherers
1984-85	Gillette Cup Winner	HKCC Witherers
1984-85	Rothmans Cup Runners Up	HKCC Optimists
1985-86	Gillette Plate Runners Up	HKCC Gap Ramblers
1986-87	Sunday League Runners Up	HKCC Scorpions
1986-87	Saturday League Runners Up	HKCC Witherers
1986-87	Gillette Cup Runners Up	HKCC Gap Ramblers
1987-88	Sunday League Winner	HKCC Wanderers
1987-88	Rothmans Cup Winner	HKCC Wanderers
1988-89	Saturday League Winner	HKCC Nomads

53 / 200 Hong Kong Cricket Club. - Chato